# The Private Pa
# Henry Rye

George Gissing

**Alpha Editions**

This edition published in 2024

ISBN 9789362511492

Design and Setting By
**Alpha Editions**
www.alphaedis.com
Email - info@alphaedis.com

# Contents

# PREFACE

The name of Henry Ryecroft never became familiar to what is called the reading public. A year ago obituary paragraphs in the literary papers gave such account of him as was thought needful: the date and place of his birth, the names of certain books he had written, an allusion to his work in the periodicals, the manner of his death. At the time it sufficed. Even those few who knew the man, and in a measure understood him, must have felt that his name called for no further celebration; like other mortals, he had lived and laboured; like other mortals, he had entered into his rest. To me, however, fell the duty of examining Ryecroft's papers; and having, in the exercise of my discretion, decided to print this little volume, I feel that it requires a word or two of biographical complement, just so much personal detail as may point the significance of the self-revelation here made.

When first I knew him, Ryecroft had reached his fortieth year; for twenty years he had lived by the pen. He was a struggling man, beset by poverty and other circumstances very unpropitious to mental work. Many forms of literature had he tried; in none had he been conspicuously successful; yet now and then he had managed to earn a little more money than his actual needs demanded, and thus was enabled to see something of foreign countries. Naturally a man of independent and rather scornful outlook, he had suffered much from defeated ambition, from disillusions of many kinds, from subjection to grim necessity; the result of it, at the time of which I am speaking, was, certainly not a broken spirit, but a mind and temper so sternly disciplined, that, in ordinary intercourse with him, one did not know but that he led a calm, contented life. Only after several years of friendship was I able to form a just idea of what the man had gone through, or of his actual existence. Little by little Ryecroft had subdued himself to a modestly industrious routine. He did a great deal of mere hack-work; he reviewed, he translated, he wrote articles; at long intervals a volume appeared under his name. There were times, I have no doubt, when bitterness took hold upon him; not seldom he suffered in health, and probably as much from moral as from physical over-strain; but, on the whole, he earned his living very much as other men do, taking the day's toil as a matter of course, and rarely grumbling over it.

Time went on; things happened; but Ryecroft was still laborious and poor. In moments of depression he spoke of his declining energies, and evidently suffered under a haunting fear of the future. The thought of dependence had always been intolerable to him; perhaps the only boast I at any time heard from his lips was that he had never incurred debt. It was a bitter thought that, after so long and hard a struggle with unkindly circumstance, he might end his life as one of the defeated.

A happier lot was in store for him. At the age of fifty, just when his health had begun to fail and his energies to show abatement, Ryecroft had the rare good fortune to find himself suddenly released from toil, and to enter upon a period of such tranquillity of mind and condition as he had never dared to hope. On the death of an acquaintance, more his friend than he imagined, the wayworn man of letters learnt with astonishment that there was bequeathed to him a life annuity of three hundred pounds. Having only himself to support (he had been a widower for several years, and his daughter, an only child, was married), Ryecroft saw in this income something more than a competency. In a few weeks he quitted the London suburb where of late he had been living, and, turning to the part of England which he loved best, he presently established himself in a cottage near Exeter, where, with a rustic housekeeper to look after him, he was soon thoroughly at home. Now and then some friend went down into Devon to see him; those who had that pleasure will not forget the plain little house amid its half-wild garden, the cosy book-room with its fine view across the valley of the Exe to Haldon, the host's cordial, gleeful hospitality, rambles with him in lanes and meadows, long talks amid the stillness of the rural night. We hoped it would all last for many a year; it seemed, indeed, as though Ryecroft had only need of rest and calm to become a hale man. But already, though he did not know it, he was suffering from a disease of the heart, which cut short his life after little more than a lustrum of quiet contentment. It had always been his wish to die suddenly; he dreaded the thought of illness, chiefly because of the trouble it gave to others. On a summer evening, after a long walk in very hot weather, he lay down upon the sofa in his study, and there—as his calm face declared—passed from slumber into the great silence.

When he left London, Ryecroft bade farewell to authorship. He told me that he hoped never to write another line for publication. But, among the papers which I looked through after his death, I came upon three manuscript books which at first glance seemed to be a diary; a date on the opening page of one of them showed that it had been begun not very long after the writer's settling in Devon. When I had read a little in these pages, I saw that they were no mere record of day-to-day life; evidently finding himself unable to forego altogether the use of the pen, the veteran had set down, as humour bade him, a thought, a reminiscence, a bit of reverie, a description of his state of mind, and so on, dating such passage merely with the month in which it was written. Sitting in the room where I had often been his companion, I turned page after page, and at moments it was as though my friend's voice sounded to me once more. I saw his worn visage, grave or smiling; recalled his familiar pose or gesture. But in this written gossip he revealed himself more intimately than in our conversation of the days gone by. Ryecroft had never erred by lack of reticence; as was natural in a sensitive man who had suffered much, he inclined to gentle acquiescence, shrank from argument, from self-assertion. Here he spoke to me without restraint, and, when I had read it all through, I knew the man better than before.

Assuredly, this writing was not intended for the public, and yet, in many a passage, I seemed to perceive the literary purpose—something more than the turn of phrase, and so on, which results from long habit of composition. Certain of his reminiscences, in particular, Ryecroft could hardly have troubled to write down had he not, however vaguely, entertained the thought of putting them to some use. I suspect that, in his happy leisure, there grew upon him a desire to write one more book, a book which should be written merely for his own satisfaction. Plainly, it would have been the best he had it in him to do. But he seems never to have attempted the arrangement of these fragmentary pieces, and probably because he could not decide upon the form they should take. I imagine him shrinking from the thought of a first-person volume; he would feel it too pretentious; he would bid himself wait for the day of riper wisdom. And so the pen fell from his hand.

Conjecturing thus, I wondered whether the irregular diary might not have wider interest than at first appeared. To me, its personal appeal was very strong; might it not be possible to cull from it the substance of a small volume which, at least for its sincerity's sake, would not be without value for those who read, not with the eye alone, but with the mind? I turned the pages again. Here was a man who, having his desire, and that a very modest one, not only felt satisfied, but enjoyed great happiness. He talked of many different things, saying exactly what he thought; he spoke of himself, and told the truth as far as mortal can tell it. It seemed to me that the thing had human interest. I decided to print.

The question of arrangement had to be considered; I did not like to offer a mere incondite miscellany. To supply each of the disconnected passages with a title, or even to group them under subject headings, would have interfered with the spontaneity which, above all, I wished to preserve. In reading through the matter I had selected, it struck me how often the aspects of nature were referred to, and how suitable many of the reflections were to the month with which they were dated. Ryecroft, I knew, had ever been much influenced by the mood of the sky, and by the procession of the year. So I hit upon the thought of dividing the little book into four chapters, named after the seasons. Like all classifications, it is imperfect, but 'twill serve.

G. G.

# SPRING

## I.

For more than a week my pen has lain untouched. I have written nothing for seven whole days, not even a letter. Except during one or two bouts of illness, such a thing never happened in my life before. In my life; the life, that is, which had to be supported by anxious toil; the life which was not lived for living's sake, as all life should be, but under the goad of fear. The earning of money should be a means to an end; for more than thirty years—I began to support myself at sixteen—I had to regard it as the end itself.

I could imagine that my old penholder feels reproachfully towards me. Has it not served me well? Why do I, in my happiness, let it lie there neglected, gathering dust? The same penholder that has lain against my forefinger day after day, for—how many years? Twenty, at least; I remember buying it at a shop in Tottenham Court Road. By the same token I bought that day a paper-weight, which cost me a whole shilling—an extravagance which made me tremble. The penholder shone with its new varnish, now it is plain brown wood from end to end. On my forefinger it has made a callosity.

Old companion, yet old enemy! How many a time have I taken it up, loathing the necessity, heavy in head and heart, my hand shaking, my eyes sick-dazzled! How I dreaded the white page I had to foul with ink! Above all, on days such as this, when the blue eyes of Spring laughed from between rosy clouds, when the sunlight shimmered upon my table and made me long, long all but to madness, for the scent of the flowering earth, for the green of hillside larches, for the singing of the skylark above the downs. There was a time—it seems further away than childhood—when I took up my pen with eagerness; if my hand trembled it was with hope. But a hope that fooled me, for never a page of my writing deserved to live. I can say that now without bitterness. It was youthful error, and only the force of circumstance prolonged it. The world has done me no injustice; thank Heaven I have grown wise enough not to rail at it for this! And why should any man who writes, even if he write things immortal, nurse anger at the world's neglect? Who asked him to publish? Who promised him a hearing? Who has broken faith with him? If my shoemaker turn me out an excellent pair of boots, and I, in some mood of cantankerous unreason, throw them back upon his hands, the man has just cause of complaint. But your poem, your novel, who bargained with you for it? If it is honest journeywork, yet lacks purchasers, at most you may call yourself a hapless tradesman. If it come from on high, with what decency do you fret and fume because it is not paid for in heavy cash? For the work of man's mind there is one test, and one alone, the judgment of generations yet unborn. If you have written a great book, the world to come will know of it. But you don't care for posthumous glory. You want to enjoy fame in a comfortable armchair. Ah, that is quite another thing. Have the courage of your desire. Admit yourself a merchant, and protest to gods and men that the merchandise you offer is of better quality than much which sells for a high price. You may be right, and indeed it is hard upon you that Fashion does not turn to your stall.

## II.

The exquisite quiet of this room! I have been sitting in utter idleness, watching the sky, viewing the shape of golden sunlight upon the carpet, which changes as the minutes pass, letting my eye wander from one framed print to another, and along the ranks of my beloved books. Within the house nothing stirs. In the garden I can hear singing of birds, I can hear the rustle of their wings. And thus, if it please me, I may sit all day long, and into the profounder quiet of the night.

My house is perfect. By great good fortune I have found a housekeeper no less to my mind, a low-voiced, light-footed woman of discreet age, strong and deft enough to render me all the service I require, and not afraid of solitude. She rises very early. By my breakfast-time there remains little to be done under the roof save dressing of meals. Very rarely do I hear even a clink of crockery; never the closing of a door or window. Oh, blessed silence!

There is not the remotest possibility of any one's calling upon me, and that I should call upon any one else is a thing undreamt of. I owe a letter to a friend; perhaps I shall write it before bedtime; perhaps I shall leave it till to-morrow morning. A letter of friendship should never be written save when the spirit prompts. I have not yet looked at the newspaper. Generally I leave it till I come back tired from my walk; it amuses me then to see what the noisy world is doing, what new self-torments men have discovered, what new forms of vain toil, what new occasions of peril and of strife. I grudge to give the first freshness of the morning mind to things so sad and foolish.

My house is perfect. Just large enough to allow the grace of order in domestic circumstance; just that superfluity of intramural space, to lack which is to be less than at one's ease. The fabric is sound; the work in wood and plaster tells of a more leisurely and a more honest age than ours. The stairs do not creak under my step; I am waylaid by no unkindly draught; I can open or close a window without muscle-ache. As to such trifles as the tint and device of wall-paper, I confess my indifference; be the walls only unobtrusive, and I am satisfied. The first thing in one's home is comfort; let beauty of detail be added if one has the means, the patience, the eye.

To me, this little book-room is beautiful, and chiefly because it is home. Through the greater part of life I was homeless. Many places have I inhabited, some which my soul loathed, and some which pleased me well; but never till now with that sense of security which makes a home. At any moment I might have been driven forth by evil hap, by nagging necessity. For all that time did I say within myself: Some day, perchance, I shall have a home; yet the "perchance" had more and more of emphasis as life went on, and at the moment when fate was secretly smiling on me, I had all but abandoned hope. I have my home at last. When I place a new volume on my shelves, I say: Stand there whilst I have eyes to see you; and a joyous tremor thrills me. This house is mine on a lease of a score of years. So long I certainly shall not live; but, if I did, even so long should I have the wherewithal to pay my rent and buy my food.

I think with compassion of the unhappy mortals for whom no such sun will ever rise. I should like to add to the Litany a new petition: "For all inhabitants of great towns, and especially for all such as dwell in lodgings, boarding-houses, flats, or any other sordid substitute for Home which need or foolishness may have contrived."

In vain I have pondered the Stoic virtues. I know that it is folly to fret about the spot of one's abode on this little earth.

> All places that the eye of heaven visits
> Are to the wise man ports and happy havens.

But I have always worshipped wisdom afar off. In the sonorous period of the philosopher, in the golden measure of the poet, I find it of all things lovely. To its possession I shall never attain. What will it serve me to pretend a virtue of which I am incapable? To me the place and manner of my abode is of supreme import; let it be confessed, and there an end of it. I am no cosmopolite. Were I to think that I should die away from England, the thought would be dreadful to me. And in England, this is the dwelling of my choice; this is my home.

### III.

I am no botanist, but I have long found pleasure in herb-gathering. I love to come upon a plant which is unknown to me, to identify it with the help of my book, to greet it by name when next it shines beside my path. If the plant be rare, its discovery gives me joy. Nature, the great Artist, makes her common flowers in the common view; no word in human language can express the marvel and the loveliness even of what we call the vulgarest weed, but these are fashioned under the gaze of every passer-by. The rare flower is shaped apart, in places secret, in the Artist's subtler mood; to find it is to enjoy the sense of admission to a holier precinct. Even in my gladness I am awed.

To-day I have walked far, and at the end of my walk I found the little white-flowered wood-ruff. It grew in a copse of young ash. When I had looked long at the flower, I delighted myself with the grace of the slim trees about it—their shining smoothness, their olive hue. Hard by stood a bush of wych elm; its tettered bark, overlined as if with the character of some unknown tongue, made the young ashes yet more beautiful.

It matters not how long I wander. There is no task to bring me back; no one will be vexed or uneasy, linger I ever so late. Spring is shining upon these lanes and meadows; I feel as if I must follow every winding track that opens by my way. Spring has restored to me something of the long-forgotten vigour of youth; I walk without weariness; I sing to myself like a boy, and the song is one I knew in boyhood.

That reminds me of an incident. Near a hamlet, in a lonely spot by a woodside, I came upon a little lad of perhaps ten years old, who, his head hidden in his arms against a tree trunk, was crying bitterly. I asked him what was the matter, and, after a little trouble—he was better than a mere bumpkin—I learnt that, having been sent with sixpence to pay a debt, he had lost the money. The poor little fellow was in a state of mind which in a grave man would be called the anguish of despair; he must have been crying for a long time; every muscle in his face quivered as if under torture, his limbs shook; his eyes, his voice, uttered such misery as only the vilest criminal should be made to suffer. And it was because he had lost sixpence!

I could have shed tears with him—tears of pity and of rage at all this spectacle implied. On a day of indescribable glory, when earth and heaven shed benedictions upon the soul of man, a child, whose nature would have bidden him rejoice as only childhood may, wept his heart out because his hand had dropped a sixpenny piece! The loss was a very serious one, and he knew it; he was less afraid to face his parents, than overcome by misery at the thought of the harm he had done them. Sixpence dropped by the wayside, and a whole family made wretched! What are the due descriptive terms for a state of "civilization" in which such a thing as this is possible?

I put my hand into my pocket, and wrought sixpennyworth of miracle.

It took me half an hour to recover my quiet mind. After all, it is as idle to rage against man's fatuity as to hope that he will ever be less a fool. For me, the great thing was my sixpenny miracle. Why, I have known the day when it would have been beyond my power altogether, or else would have cost me a meal. Wherefore, let me again be glad and thankful.

## IV.

There was a time in my life when, if I had suddenly been set in the position I now enjoy, conscience would have lain in ambush for me. What! An income sufficient to support three or four working-class families—a house all to myself—things beautiful wherever I turn—and absolutely nothing to do for it all! I should have been hard put to it to defend myself. In those days I was feelingly reminded, hour by hour, with what a struggle the obscure multitudes manage to keep alive. Nobody knows better than I do *quam parvo liceat producere vitam.* I have hungered in the streets; I have laid my head in the poorest shelter; I know what it is to feel the heart burn with wrath and envy of "the privileged classes." Yes, but all that time I was one of "the privileged" myself, and now I can accept a recognized standing among them without shadow of self-reproach.

It does not mean that my larger sympathies are blunted. By going to certain places, looking upon certain scenes, I could most effectually destroy all the calm that life has brought me. If I hold apart and purposely refuse to look that way, it is because I believe that the world is better, not worse, for having one more inhabitant who lives as becomes a civilized being. Let him whose soul prompts him to assail the iniquity of things, cry and spare not; let him who has the vocation go forth and combat. In me it would be to err from Nature's guidance. I know, if I know anything, that I am made for the life of tranquillity and meditation. I know that only thus can such virtue as I possess find scope. More than half a century of existence has taught me that most of the wrong and folly which darken earth is due to those who cannot possess their souls in quiet; that most of the good which saves mankind from destruction comes of life that is led in thoughtful stillness. Every day the world grows noisier; I, for one, will have no part in that increasing clamour, and, were it only by my silence, I confer a boon on all.

How well would the revenues of a country be expended, if, by mere pensioning, one-fifth of its population could be induced to live as I do!

## V.

"Sir," said Johnson, "all the arguments which are brought to represent poverty as no evil, show it to be evidently a great evil. You never find people labouring to convince you that you may live very happily upon a plentiful fortune."

He knew what he was talking of, that rugged old master of common sense. Poverty is of course a relative thing; the term has reference, above all, to one's standing as an intellectual being. If I am to believe the newspapers, there are title-bearing men and women in England who, had they an assured income of five-and-twenty, shillings per week, would have no right to call themselves poor, for their intellectual needs are those of a stable-boy or scullery wench. Give me the same income and I can live, but I am poor indeed.

You tell me that money cannot buy the things most precious. Your commonplace proves that you have never known the lack of it. When I think of all the sorrow and the barrenness that has been wrought in my life by want of a few more pounds per annum than I was able to earn, I stand aghast at money's significance. What kindly joys have I lost, those simple forms of happiness to which every heart has claim, because of poverty! Meetings with those I loved made impossible year after year; sadness, misunderstanding, nay, cruel alienation, arising from inability to do the things I wished, and which I might have done had a little money helped me; endless instances of homely pleasure and contentment curtailed or forbidden by narrow means. I have lost friends merely through the constraints of my position; friends I might have made have remained strangers to me; solitude of the bitter kind, the solitude which is enforced at times when mind or heart longs for companionship, often cursed my life solely because I was poor. I think it would scarce be an exaggeration to say that there is no moral good which has not to be paid for in coin of the realm.

"Poverty," said Johnson again, "is so great an evil, and pregnant with so much temptation, so much misery, that I cannot but earnestly enjoin you to avoid it."

For my own part, I needed no injunction to that effort of avoidance. Many a London garret knows how I struggled with the unwelcome chamber-fellow. I marvel she did not abide with me to the end; it is a sort of inconsequence in Nature, and sometimes makes me vaguely uneasy through nights of broken sleep.

## VI.

How many more springs can I hope to see? A sanguine temper would say ten or twelve; let me dare to hope humbly for five or six. That is a great many. Five or six spring-times, welcomed joyously, lovingly watched from the first celandine to the budding of the rose; who shall dare to call it a stinted boon? Five or six times the miracle of earth reclad, the vision of splendour and loveliness which tongue has never yet described, set before my gazing. To think of it is to fear that I ask too much.

## VII.

"Homo animal querulum cupide suis incumbens miseriis." I wonder where that comes from. I found it once in Charron, quoted without reference, and it has often been in my mind—a dreary truth, well worded. At least, it was a truth for me during many a long year. Life, I fancy, would very often be insupportable, but for the luxury of self-compassion; in cases numberless, this it must be that saves from suicide. For some there is great relief in talking about their miseries, but such gossips lack the profound solace of misery nursed in silent brooding. Happily, the trick with me has never been retrospective; indeed, it was never, even with regard to instant suffering, a habit so deeply rooted as to become a mastering vice. I knew my own weakness when I yielded to it; I despised myself when it brought me comfort; I could laugh scornfully, even "cupide meis incumbens miseriis." And now, thanks be to the unknown power which rules us, my past has buried its dead. More than that; I can accept with sober cheerfulness the necessity of all I lived through. So it was to be; so it was. For this did Nature shape me; with what purpose, I shall never know; but, in the sequence of things eternal, this was my place.

Could I have achieved so much philosophy if, as I ever feared, the closing years of my life had passed in helpless indigence? Should I not have sunk into lowest depths of querulous self-pity, grovelling there with eyes obstinately averted from the light above?

## VIII.

The early coming of spring in this happy Devon gladdens my heart. I think with chill discomfort of those parts of England where the primrose shivers beneath a sky of threat rather than of solace. Honest winter, snow-clad and with the frosted beard, I can welcome not uncordially; but that long deferment of the calendar's promise, that weeping gloom of March and April, that bitter blast outraging the honour of May—how often has it robbed me of heart and hope. Here, scarce have I assured myself that the last leaf has fallen, scarce have I watched the glistening of hoar-frost upon the evergreens, when a breath from the west thrills me with anticipation of bud and bloom. Even under this grey-billowing sky, which tells that February is still in rule:—

> Mild winds shake the elder brake,
> And the wandering herdsmen know
> That the whitethorn soon will blow.

I have been thinking of those early years of mine in London, when the seasons passed over me unobserved, when I seldom turned a glance towards the heavens, and felt no hardship in the imprisonment of boundless streets. It is strange now to remember that for some six or seven years I never looked upon a meadow, never travelled even so far as to the tree-bordered suburbs. I was battling for dear life; on most days I could not feel certain that in a week's time I should have food and shelter. It would happen, to be sure, that in hot noons of August my thoughts wandered to the sea; but so impossible was the gratification of such desire that it never greatly troubled me. At times, indeed, I seem all but to have forgotten that people went away for holiday. In those poor parts of the town where I dwelt, season made no perceptible difference; there were no luggage-laden cabs to remind me of joyous journeys; the folk about me went daily to their toil as usual, and so did I. I remember afternoons of languor, when books were a weariness, and no thought could be squeezed out of the drowsy brain; then would I betake myself to one of the parks, and find refreshment without any enjoyable sense of change. Heavens, how I laboured in those days! And how far I was from thinking of myself as a subject for compassion! That came later, when my health had begun to suffer from excess of toil, from bad air, bad food and many miseries; then awoke the maddening desire for countryside and sea-beach—and for other things yet more remote. But in the years when I toiled hardest and underwent what now appear to me hideous privations, of a truth I could not be said to suffer at all. I did not suffer, for I had no sense of weakness. My health was proof against everything, and my energies defied all malice of circumstance. With however little encouragement, I had infinite hope. Sound sleep (often in places I now dread to think of) sent me fresh to the battle each morning, my breakfast, sometimes, no more than a slice of bread and a cup of water. As human happiness goes, I am not sure that I was not then happy.

Most men who go through a hard time in their youth are supported by companionship. London has no *pays latin*, but hungry beginners in literature have generally their suitable comrades, garreteers in the Tottenham Court Road district, or in unredeemed Chelsea; they make their little *vie de Bohème*, and are consciously proud of it. Of my position, the peculiarity was that I never belonged to any cluster; I shrank from casual acquaintance, and, through the grim years, had but one friend with whom I held converse. It was never my instinct to look for help, to seek favour for advancement; whatever step I gained was gained by my own strength. Even as I disregarded favour so did I scorn advice; no counsel would I ever take but that of my own brain and heart. More than once I was driven by necessity to beg from strangers the means of earning bread, and this of all my experiences was the bitterest; yet I think I should have found it worse still to incur a debt to some friend or comrade. The truth is that I have never learnt to regard myself as a "member of society." For me, there have always been two entities—myself and the world, and the normal relation between these two has been hostile. Am I not still a lonely man, as far as ever from forming part of the social order?

This, of which I once was scornfully proud, seems to me now, if not a calamity, something I would not choose if life were to live again.

## IX.

For more than six years I trod the pavement, never stepping once upon mother earth—for the parks are but pavement disguised with a growth of grass. Then the worst was over. Say I the worst? No, no; things far worse were to come; the struggle against starvation has its cheery side when one is young and vigorous. But at all events I had begun to earn a living; I held assurance of food and clothing for half a year at a time; granted health, I might hope to draw my not insufficient wages for many a twelvemonth. And they were the wages of work done independently, when and where I would. I thought with horror of lives spent in an office, with an employer to obey. The glory of the career of letters was its freedom, its dignity!

The fact of the matter was, of course, that I served, not one master, but a whole crowd of them. Independence, forsooth! If my writing failed to please editor, publisher, public, where was my daily bread? The greater my success, the more numerous my employers. I was the slave of a multitude. By heaven's grace I had succeeded in pleasing (that is to say, in making myself a source of profit to) certain persons who represented this vague throng; for the time, they were gracious to me; but what justified me in the faith that I should hold the ground I had gained? Could the position of any toiling man be more precarious than mine? I tremble now as I think of it, tremble as I should in watching some one who walked carelessly on the edge of an abyss. I marvel at the recollection that for a good score of years this pen and a scrap of paper clothed and fed me and my household, kept me in physical comfort, held at bay all those hostile forces of the world ranged against one who has no resource save in his own right hand.

But I was thinking of the year which saw my first exodus from London. On an irresistible impulse, I suddenly made up my mind to go into Devon, a part of England I had never seen. At the end of March I escaped from my grim lodgings, and, before I had time to reflect on the details of my undertaking, I found myself sitting in sunshine at a spot very near to where I now dwell—before me the green valley of the broadening Exe and the pine-clad ridge of Haldon. That was one of the moments of my life when I have tasted exquisite joy. My state of mind was very strange. Though as boy and youth I had been familiar with the country, had seen much of

England's beauties, it was as though I found myself for the first time before a natural landscape. Those years of London had obscured all my earlier life; I was like a man town-born and bred, who scarce knows anything but street vistas. The light, the air, had for me something of the supernatural—affected me, indeed, only less than at a later time did the atmosphere of Italy. It was glorious spring weather; a few white clouds floated amid the blue, and the earth had an intoxicating fragrance. Then first did I know myself for a sun-worshipper. How had I lived so long without asking whether there was a sun in the heavens or not? Under that radiant firmament, I could have thrown myself upon my knees in adoration. As I walked, I found myself avoiding every strip of shadow; were it but that of a birch trunk, I felt as if it robbed me of the day's delight. I went bare-headed, that the golden beams might shed upon me their unstinted blessing. That day I must have walked some thirty miles, yet I knew not fatigue. Could I but have once more the strength which then supported me!

I had stepped into a new life. Between the man I had been and that which I now became there was a very notable difference. In a single day I had matured astonishingly; which means, no doubt, that I suddenly entered into conscious enjoyment of powers and sensibilities which had been developing unknown to me. To instance only one point: till then I had cared very little about plants and flowers, but now I found myself eagerly interested in every blossom, in every growth of the wayside. As I walked I gathered a quantity of plants, promising myself to buy a book on the morrow and identify them all. Nor was it a passing humour; never since have I lost my pleasure in the flowers of the field, and my desire to know them all. My ignorance at the time of which I speak seems to me now very shameful; but I was merely in the case of ordinary people, whether living in town or country. How many could give the familiar name of half a dozen plants plucked at random from beneath the hedge in springtime? To me the flowers became symbolical of a great release, of a wonderful awakening. My eyes had all at once been opened; till then I had walked in darkness, yet knew it not.

Well do I remember the rambles of that springtide. I had a lodging in one of those outer streets of Exeter which savour more of country than of town, and every morning I set forth to make discoveries. The weather could not have been more kindly; I felt the influences of a climate I had never known; there was a balm in the air which soothed no less than it exhilarated me. Now inland, now seaward, I followed the windings of the Exe. One day I wandered in rich, warm valleys, by orchards bursting into bloom, from farmhouse to farmhouse, each more beautiful than the other, and from hamlet to hamlet bowered amid dark evergreens; the next, I was on pine-clad heights, gazing over moorland brown with last year's heather, feeling upon my face a wind from the white-flecked Channel. So intense was my delight in the beautiful world about me that I forgot even myself; I enjoyed without retrospect or forecast; I, the egoist in grain, forgot to scrutinize my own emotions, or to trouble my happiness by comparison with others' happier fortune. It was a healthful time; it gave me a new lease of life, and taught me—in so far as I was teachable—how to make use of it.

## X.

Mentally and physically, I must be much older than my years. At three-and-fifty a man ought not to be brooding constantly on his vanished youth. These days of spring which I should be enjoying for their own sake, do but turn me to reminiscence, and my memories are of the springs that were lost.

Some day I will go to London and revisit all the places where I housed in the time of my greatest poverty. I have not seen them for a quarter of a century or so. Not long ago, had any one asked me how I felt about these memories, I should have said that there were certain street names, certain mental images of obscure London, which made me wretched as often as they came before me; but, in truth, it is a very long time since I was moved to any sort of bitterness by that retrospect of things hard and squalid. Now, owning all the misery of it in comparison with what should have been, I find that part of life interesting and pleasant to look back upon— greatly more so than many subsequent times, when I lived amid decencies and had enough to eat. Some day I will go to London, and spend a day or two amid the dear old horrors. Some of the places, I know, have disappeared. I see the winding way by which I went from Oxford Street, at the foot of Tottenham Court Road, to Leicester Square, and, somewhere in the labyrinth (I think of it as always foggy and gas-lit) was a shop which had pies and puddings in the window, puddings and pies kept hot by steam rising through perforated metal. How many a time have I stood there, raging with hunger, unable to purchase even one pennyworth of food! The shop and the street have long since vanished; does any man remember them so feelingly as I? But I think most of my haunts are still in existence: to tread again those pavements, to look at those grimy doorways and purblind windows, would affect me strangely.

I see that alley hidden on the west side of Tottenham Court Road, where, after living in a back bedroom on the top floor, I had to exchange for the front cellar; there was a difference, if I remember rightly, of sixpence a week, and sixpence, in those days, was a very great consideration—why, it meant a couple of meals. (I once *found* sixpence in the street, and had an exultation which is vivid in me at this moment.) The front cellar was stone-floored; its furniture was a table, a chair, a wash-stand, and a bed; the window, which of course had never been cleaned since it was put in, received light through a flat grating in the alley above. Here I lived; here *I wrote*. Yes, "literary work" was done at that filthy deal table, on which, by the bye, lay my Homer, my Shakespeare, and the few other books I then possessed. At night, as I lay in bed, I used to hear the tramp, tramp of a *posse* of policemen who passed along the alley on their way to relieve guard; their heavy feet sometimes sounded on the grating above my window.

I recall a tragi-comical incident of life at the British Museum. Once, on going down into the lavatory to wash my hands, I became aware of a notice newly set up above the row of basins. It ran somehow thus: "Readers are requested to bear in mind that these basins are to be used only for casual ablutions." Oh, the significance of that inscription! Had I not myself, more than once, been glad to use this soap and water more largely than the sense of the authorities contemplated? And there were poor fellows working under the great dome whose need, in this respect, was greater than mine. I laughed heartily at the notice, but it meant so much.

Some of my abodes I have utterly forgotten; for one reason or another, I was always moving—an easy matter when all my possessions lay in one small trunk. Sometimes the people of the house were intolerable. In those days I was not fastidious, and I seldom had any but the slightest intercourse with those who dwelt under the same roof, yet it happened now and then that I was driven away by human proximity which passed my endurance. In other cases I had to flee from pestilential conditions. How I escaped mortal illness in some of those places (miserably fed as I always was, and always over-working myself) is a great mystery. The worst that befell me was a slight attack of diphtheria—traceable, I imagine, to the existence of a dust-bin *under the staircase*. When I spoke of the matter to my landlady, she was at first astonished, then wrathful, and my departure was expedited with many insults.

On the whole, however, I had nothing much to complain of except my poverty. You cannot expect great comfort in London for four-and-sixpence a week—the most I ever could pay for a "furnished room with attendance" in those days of pretty stern apprenticeship. And I was easily satisfied; I wanted only a little walled space in which I could seclude myself, free from external annoyance. Certain comforts of civilized life I ceased even to regret; a stair-carpet I regarded as rather extravagant, and a carpet on the floor of my room was luxury undreamt of. My sleep was sound; I have passed nights of dreamless repose on beds which it would now make my bones ache only to look at. A door that locked, a fire in winter, a pipe of tobacco—these were things essential; and, granted these, I have been often richly contented in the squalidest garret. One such lodging is often in my memory; it was at Islington, not far from the City Road; my window looked upon the Regent's Canal. As often as I think of it, I recall what was perhaps the worst London fog I ever knew; for three successive days, at least, my lamp had to be kept burning; when I looked through the window, I saw, at moments, a few blurred lights in the street beyond the Canal, but for the most part nothing but a yellowish darkness, which caused the glass to reflect the firelight and my own face. Did I feel miserable? Not a bit of it. The enveloping gloom seemed to make my chimney-corner only the more cosy. I had coals, oil, tobacco in sufficient quantity; I had a book to read; I had work which interested me; so I went forth only to get my meals at a City Road coffee-shop, and hastened back to the fireside. Oh, my ambitions, my hopes! How surprised and indignant I should have felt had I known of any one who pitied me!

Nature took revenge now and then. In winter time I had fierce sore throats, sometimes accompanied by long and savage headaches. Doctoring, of course, never occurred to me; I just locked my door, and, if I felt very bad indeed, went to bed—to lie there, without food or drink, till I was able to look after myself again. I could never ask from a landlady anything which was not in our bond, and only once or twice did I receive spontaneous offer of help. Oh, it is wonderful to think of all that youth can endure! What a poor feeble wretch I now seem to myself, when I remember thirty years ago!

## XI.

Would I live it over again, that life of the garret and the cellar? Not with the assurance of fifty years' contentment such as I now enjoy to follow upon it! With man's infinitely pathetic power of resignation, one sees the thing on its better side, forgets all the worst of it, makes out a case for the resolute optimist. Oh, but the waste of energy, of zeal, of youth! In another mood, I could shed tears over that spectacle of rare vitality condemned to sordid strife. The pity of it! And—if our conscience mean anything at all—the bitter wrong!

Without seeking for Utopia, think what a man's youth might be. I suppose not one in every thousand uses half the possibilities of natural joy and delightful effort which lie in those years between seventeen and seven-and-twenty. All but all men have to look back upon beginnings of life deformed and discoloured by necessity, accident, wantonness. If a young man avoid the grosser pitfalls, if he keep his eye fixed steadily on what is called the main chance, if, without flagrant selfishness, he prudently subdue every interest to his own (by "interest" understanding only material good), he is putting his youth to profit, he is an exemplar and a subject of pride. I doubt whether, in our civilization, any other ideal is easy of pursuit by the youngster face to face with life. It is the only course altogether safe. Yet compare it with what might be, if men respected manhood, if human reason were at the service of human happiness. Some few there are who can look back upon a boyhood of natural delights, followed by a decade or so of fine energies honourably put to use, blended therewith, perhaps, a memory of joy so exquisite that it tunes all life unto the end; they are almost as rare as poets. The vast majority think not of their youth at all, or, glancing backward, are unconscious of lost opportunity, unaware of degradation suffered. Only by contrast with this thick-witted multitude can I pride myself upon my youth of endurance and of combat. I had a goal before me, and not the goal of the average man. Even when pinched with hunger, I did not abandon my purposes, which were of the mind. But contrast that starved lad in his slum lodging with any fair conception of intelligent and zealous youth, and one feels that a dose of swift poison would have been the right remedy for such squalid ills.

## XII.

As often as I survey my bookshelves I am reminded of Lamb's "ragged veterans." Not that all my volumes came from the second-hand stall; many of them were neat enough in new covers, some were even stately in fragrant bindings, when they passed into my hands. But so often have I removed, so rough has been the treatment of my little library at each change of place, and, to tell the truth, so little care have I given to its well-being at normal times (for in all practical matters I am idle and inept), that even the comeliest of my books show the results of unfair usage. More than one has been foully injured by a great nail driven into a packing-case— this but the extreme instance of the wrongs they have undergone. Now that I have leisure and peace of mind, I find myself growing more careful— an illustration of the great truth that virtue is made easy by circumstance. But I confess that, so long as a volume hold together, I am not much troubled as to its outer appearance.

I know men who say they had as lief read any book in a library copy as in one from their own shelf. To me that is unintelligible. For one thing, I know every book of mine by its *scent*, and I have but to put my nose between the pages to be reminded of all sorts of things. My Gibbon, for example, my well-bound eight-volume Milman edition, which I have read and read and read again for more than thirty years—never do I open it but the scent of the noble page restores to me all the exultant happiness of that moment when I received it as a prize. Or my Shakespeare, the great Cambridge Shakespeare—it has an odour which carries me yet further back in life; for these volumes belonged to my father, and before I was old enough to read them with understanding, it was often permitted me, as a treat, to take down one of them from the bookcase, and reverently to turn the leaves. The volumes smell exactly as they did in that old time, and what a strange tenderness comes upon me when I hold one of them in hand. For that reason I do not often read Shakespeare in this edition. My eyes being good as ever, I take the Globe volume, which I bought in days when such a purchase was something more than an extravagance; wherefore I regard the book with that peculiar affection which results from sacrifice.

Sacrifice—in no drawing-room sense of the word. Dozens of my books were purchased with money which ought to have been spent upon what are called the necessaries of life. Many a time I have stood before a stall, or a bookseller's window, torn by conflict of intellectual desire and bodily need. At the very hour of dinner, when my stomach clamoured for food, I have been stopped by sight of a volume so long coveted, and marked at so advantageous a price, that I *could* not let it go; yet to buy it meant pangs of famine. My Heyne's *Tibullus* was grasped at such a moment. It lay on the stall of the old book-shop in Goodge Street—a stall where now and then one found an excellent thing among quantities of rubbish. Sixpence was the price—sixpence! At that time I used to eat my mid-day meal (of course my dinner) at a coffee-shop in Oxford Street, one of the real old coffee-shops, such as now, I suppose, can hardly be found. Sixpence was all I had—yes, all I had in the world; it would purchase a plate of meat and vegetables. But I did not dare to hope that the *Tibullus* would wait until the morrow, when a certain small sum fell due to me. I paced the pavement, fingering the coppers in my pocket, eyeing the stall, two appetites at combat within me. The book was bought and I went home with it, and as I made a dinner of bread and butter I gloated over the pages.

In this *Tibullus* I found pencilled on the last page: "Perlegi, Oct. 4, 1792." Who was that possessor of the book, nearly a hundred years ago? There was no other inscription. I like to imagine some poor scholar, poor and eager as I myself, who bought the volume with drops of his blood, and enjoyed the reading of it even as I did. How much *that* was I could not easily say. Gentle-hearted Tibullus!—of whom there remains to us a poet's portrait more delightful, I think, than anything of the kind in Roman literature.

> An tacitum silvas inter reptare salubres,
> Curantem quidquid dignum sapiente bonoque est?

So with many another book on the thronged shelves. To take them down is to recall, how vividly, a struggle and a triumph. In those days money represented nothing to me, nothing I cared to think about, but the acquisition of books. There were books of which I had passionate need, books more necessary to me than bodily nourishment. I could see them, of course, at the British Museum, but that was not at all the same thing as having and holding them, my own property, on my own shelf. Now and then I have bought a volume of the raggedest and wretchedest aspect, dishonoured with foolish scribbling, torn, blotted—no matter, I liked better to read out of that than out of a copy that was not mine. But I was guilty at times of mere self-indulgence; a book tempted me, a book which was not one of those for which I really craved, a luxury which prudence might bid me forego. As, for instance, my *Jung-Stilling*. It caught my eye in Holywell Street; the name was familiar to me in *Wahrheit und Dichtung*, and curiosity grew as I glanced over the pages. But that day I resisted; in truth, I could not afford the eighteen-pence, which means that just then I was poor indeed. Twice again did I pass, each time assuring myself that *Jung-Stilling* had found no purchaser. There came a day when I was in funds. I see myself hastening to Holywell Street (in those days my habitual pace was five miles an hour), I see the little grey old man with whom I transacted my business—what was his name?—the bookseller who had been, I believe, a Catholic priest, and still had a certain priestly dignity about him. He took the volume, opened it, mused for a moment, then, with a glance at me, said, as if thinking aloud: "Yes, I wish I had time to read it."

Sometimes I added the labour of a porter to my fasting endured for the sake of books. At the little shop near Portland Road Station I came upon a first edition of Gibbon, the price an absurdity—I think it was a shilling a volume. To possess those clean-paged quartos I would have sold my coat. As it happened, I had not money enough with me, but sufficient at home. I was living at Islington. Having spoken with the bookseller, I walked home, took the cash, walked back again, and—carried the tomes from the west end of Euston Road to a street in Islington far beyond the *Angel*. I did it in two journeys—this being the only time in my life when I thought of Gibbon in avoirdupois. Twice—three times, reckoning the walk for the money—did I descend Euston Road and climb Pentonville on that occasion. Of the season and the weather I have no recollection; my joy in the purchase I had made drove out every other thought. Except, indeed, of the weight. I had infinite energy, but not much muscular strength, and the end of the last journey saw me upon a chair, perspiring, flaccid, aching—exultant!

The well-to-do person would hear this story with astonishment. Why did I not get the bookseller to send me the volumes? Or, if I could not wait, was there no omnibus along that London highway? How could I make the well-to-do person understand that I did not feel able to afford, that day, one penny more than I had spent on the book? No, no, such labour-saving expenditure did not come within my scope; whatever I enjoyed I earned it, literally, by the sweat of my brow. In those days I hardly knew what it was to travel by omnibus. I have walked London streets for twelve and fifteen hours together without ever a thought of saving my legs, or my time, by paying for waftage. Being poor as poor can be, there were certain things I had to renounce, and this was one of them.

Years after, I sold my first edition of Gibbon for even less than it cost me; it went with a great many other fine books in folio and quarto, which I could not drag about with me in my constant removals; the man who bought them spoke of them as "tomb-stones." Why has Gibbon no market value? Often has my heart ached with regret for those quartos. The joy of reading the Decline and Fall in that fine type! The page was appropriate to the dignity of the subject; the mere sight of it tuned one's mind. I suppose I could easily get another copy now; but it would not be to me what that other was, with its memory of dust and toil.

### XIII.

There must be several men of spirit and experiences akin to mine who remember that little book-shop opposite Portland Road Station. It had a peculiar character; the books were of a solid kind—chiefly theology and classics—and for the most part those old editions which are called worthless, which have no bibliopolic value, and have been supplanted for practical use by modern issues. The bookseller was very much a gentleman, and this singular fact, together with the extremely low prices at which his volumes were marked, sometimes inclined me to think that he kept the shop for mere love of letters. Things in my eyes inestimable I have purchased there for a few pence, and I don't think I ever gave more than a shilling for any volume. As I once had the opportunity of perceiving, a young man fresh from class-rooms could only look with wondering contempt on the antiquated stuff which it rejoiced me to gather from that kindly stall, or from the richer shelves within. My *Cicero's Letters* for instance: podgy volumes in parchment, with all the notes of Graevius, Gronovius, and I know not how many other old scholars. Pooh! Hopelessly out of date. But I could never feel that. I have a deep affection for Graevius and Gronovius and the rest, and if I knew as much as they did, I should be well satisfied to rest under the young man's disdain. The zeal of learning is never out of date; the example—were there no more—burns before one as a sacred fire, for ever unquenchable. In what modern editor shall I find such love and enthusiasm as glows in the annotations of old scholars?

Even the best editions of our day have so much of the mere school-book; you feel so often that the man does not regard his author as literature, but simply as text. Pedant for pedant, the old is better than the new.

### XIV.

To-day's newspaper contains a yard or so of reading about a spring horse-race. The sight of it fills me with loathing. It brings to my mind that placard I saw at a station in Surrey a year or two ago, advertising certain races in the neighbourhood. Here is the poster, as I copied it into my note-book:

> "Engaged by the Executive to ensure order and comfort to the public attending this meeting:—
>
> 14 detectives (racing),
> 15 detectives (Scotland Yard),
> 7 police inspectors,
> 9 police sergeants,
> 76 police, and a supernumerary contingent of specially selected men from the Army Reserve and the Corps of Commissionaires.
>
> The above force will be employed solely for the purpose of maintaining order and excluding bad characters, etc. They will have the assistance also of a strong force of the Surrey Constabulary."

I remember, once, when I let fall a remark on the subject of horse-racing among friends chatting together, I was voted "morose." Is it really morose to object to public gatherings which their own promoters declare to be dangerous for all decent folk? Every one knows that horse-racing is carried on mainly for the delight and profit of fools, ruffians, and thieves. That intelligent men allow themselves to take part in the affair, and defend their conduct by declaring that their presence "maintains the character of a sport essentially noble," merely shows that intelligence can easily enough divest itself of sense and decency.

## XV.

Midway in my long walk yesterday, I lunched at a wayside inn. On the table lay a copy of a popular magazine. Glancing over this miscellany, I found an article, by a woman, on "Lion Hunting," and in this article I came upon a passage which seemed worth copying.

"As I woke my husband, the lion—which was then about forty yards off—charged straight towards us, and with my .303 I hit him full in the chest, as we afterwards discovered, tearing his windpipe to pieces and breaking his spine. He charged a second time, and the next shot hit him through the shoulder, tearing his heart to ribbons."

It would interest me to look upon this heroine of gun and pen. She is presumably quite a young woman; probably, when at home, a graceful figure in drawing-rooms. I should like to hear her talk, to exchange thoughts with her. She would give one a very good idea of the matron of old Rome who had her seat in the amphitheatre. Many of those ladies, in private life, must have been bright and gracious, high-bred and full of agreeable sentiment; they talked of art and of letters; they could drop a tear over Lesbia's sparrow; at the same time, they were connoisseurs in torn windpipes, shattered spines and viscera rent open. It is not likely that many of them would have cared to turn their own hands to butchery, and, for the matter of that, I must suppose that our Lion Huntress of the popular magazine is rather an exceptional dame; but no doubt she and the Roman ladies would get on very well together, finding only a few superficial differences. The fact that her gory reminiscences are welcomed by an editor with the popular taste in view is perhaps more significant than appears either to editor or public. Were this lady to write a novel (the chances are she will) it would have the true note of modern vigour. Of course her style has been formed by her favourite reading; more than probably, her ways of thinking and feeling owe much to the same source. If not so already, this will soon, I daresay, be the typical Englishwoman. Certainly, there is "no nonsense about her." Such women should breed a remarkable race.

I left the inn in rather a turbid humour. Moving homeward by a new way, I presently found myself on the side of a little valley, in which lay a farm and an orchard. The apple trees were in full bloom, and, as I stood gazing, the sun, which had all that day been niggard of its beams, burst forth gloriously. For what I then saw, I have no words; I can but dream of the still loveliness of that blossomed valley. Near me, a bee was humming; not far away, a cuckoo called; from the pasture of the farm below came a bleating of lambs.

## XVI.

I am no friend of the people. As a force, by which the tenor of the time is conditioned, they inspire me with distrust, with fear; as a visible multitude, they make me shrink aloof, and often move me to abhorrence. For the greater part of my life, the people signified to me the London crowd, and no phrase of temperate meaning would utter my thoughts of them under that aspect. The people as country-folk are little known to me; such glimpses as I have had of them do not invite to nearer acquaintance. Every instinct of my being is anti-democratic, and I dread to think of what our England may become when Demos rules irresistibly.

Right or wrong, this is my temper. But he who should argue from it that I am intolerant of all persons belonging to a lower social rank than my own would go far astray. Nothing is more rooted in my mind than the vast distinction between the individual and the class. Take a man by himself, and there is generally some reason to be found in him, some disposition for good; mass him with his fellows in the social organism, and ten to one he becomes a blatant creature, without a thought of his own, ready for any evil to which contagion prompts him. It is because nations tend to stupidity and baseness that mankind moves so slowly; it is because individuals have a capacity for better things that it moves at all.

In my youth, looking at this man and that, I marvelled that humanity had made so little progress. Now, looking at men in the multitude, I marvel that they have advanced so far.

Foolishly arrogant as I was, I used to judge the worth of a person by his intellectual power and attainment. I could see no good where there was no logic, no charm where there was no learning. Now I think that one has to distinguish between two forms of intelligence, that of the brain, and that of the heart, and I have come to regard the second as by far the more important. I guard myself against saying that intelligence does not matter; the fool is ever as noxious as he is wearisome. But assuredly the best people I have known were saved from folly not by the intellect but by the heart. They come before me, and I see them greatly ignorant, strongly prejudiced, capable of the absurdest mis-reasoning; yet their faces shine with the supreme virtues, kindness, sweetness, modesty, generosity. Possessing these qualities, they at the same time understand how to use them; they have the intelligence of the heart.

This poor woman who labours for me in my house is even such a one. From the first I thought her an unusually good servant; after three years of acquaintance, I find her one of the few women I have known who merit the term of excellent. She can read and write—that is all. More instruction would, I am sure, have harmed her, for it would have confused her natural motives, without supplying any clear ray of mental guidance. She is fulfilling the offices for which she was born, and that with a grace of contentment, a joy of conscientiousness, which puts her high among civilized beings. Her delight is in order and in peace; what greater praise can be given to any of the children of men?

The other day she told me a story of the days gone by. Her mother, at the age of twelve, went into domestic service; but on what conditions, think you? The girl's father, an honest labouring man, *paid* the person whose house she entered one shilling a week for her instruction in the duties she wished to undertake. What a grinning stare would come to the face of any labourer nowadays, who should be asked to do the like! I no longer wonder that my housekeeper so little resembles the average of her kind.

## XVII.

A day of almost continuous rain, yet for me a day of delight. I had breakfasted, and was poring over the map of Devon (how I love a good map!) to trace an expedition that I have in view, when a knock came at my door, and Mrs. M. bore in a great brown-paper parcel, which I saw at a glance must contain books. The order was sent to London a few days ago; I had not expected to have my books so soon. With throbbing heart I set the parcel on a clear table; eyed it whilst I mended the fire; then took my pen-knife, and gravely, deliberately, though with hand that trembled, began to unpack.

It is a joy to go through booksellers' catalogues, ticking here and there a possible purchase. Formerly, when I could seldom spare money, I kept catalogues as much as possible out of sight; now I savour them page by page, and make a pleasant virtue of the discretion I must needs impose upon myself. But greater still is the happiness of unpacking volumes which one has bought without seeing them. I am no hunter of rarities; I care nothing for first editions and for tall copies; what I buy is literature, food for the soul of man. The first glimpse of bindings when the inmost protective wrapper has been folded back! The first scent of *books*! The first gleam of a gilded title! Here is a work the name of which has been known to me for half a lifetime, but which I never yet saw; I take it reverently in my hand, gently I open it; my eyes are dim with excitement as I glance over chapter-headings, and anticipate the treat which awaits me. Who, more than I, has taken to heart that sentence of the *Imitatio*—"In omnibus requiem quaesivi, et nusquam inveni nisi in angulo cum libro"?

I had in me the making of a scholar. With leisure and tranquillity of mind, I should have amassed learning. Within the walls of a college, I should have lived so happily, so harmlessly, my imagination ever busy with the old world. In the introduction to his History of France, Michelet says: "J'ai passé à côté du monde, et j'ai pris l'histoire pour la vie." That, as I can see now, was my true ideal; through all my battlings and miseries I have always lived more in the past than in the present. At the time when I was literally starving in London, when it seemed impossible that I should ever gain a living by my pen, how many days have I spent at the British Museum, reading as disinterestedly as if I had been without a care! It astounds me to remember that, having breakfasted on dry bread, and carrying in my pocket another piece of bread to serve for dinner, I settled myself at a desk in the great Reading-Room with books before me which by no possibility could be a source of immediate profit. At such a time, I worked through German tomes on Ancient Philosophy. At such a time, I read Appuleius and Lucian, Petronius and the Greek Anthology, Diogenes Laertius and— heaven knows what! My hunger was forgotten; the garret to which I must return to pass the night never perturbed my thoughts. On the whole, it seems to me something to be rather proud of; I smile approvingly at that thin, white-faced youth. Me? My very self? No, no! He has been dead these thirty years.

Scholarship in the high sense was denied me, and now it is too late. Yet here am I gloating over Pausanias, and promising myself to read every word of him. Who that has any tincture of old letters would not like to read Pausanias, instead of mere quotations from him and references to him? Here are the volumes of Dahn's *Die Könige der Germanen*: who would not like to know all he can about the Teutonic conquerors of Rome? And so on, and so on. To the end I shall be reading—and forgetting. Ah, that's the worst of it! Had I at command all the knowledge I have at any time possessed, I might call myself a learned man. Nothing surely is so bad for the memory as long-enduring worry, agitation, fear. I cannot preserve more than a few fragments of what I read, yet read I shall, persistently, rejoicingly. Would I gather erudition for a future life? Indeed, it no longer troubles me that I forget. I have the happiness of the passing moment, and what more can mortal ask?

## XVIII.

Is it I, Henry Ryecroft, who, after a night of untroubled rest, rise unhurriedly, dress with the deliberation of an oldish man, and go downstairs happy in the thought that I can sit reading, quietly reading, all day long? Is it I, Henry Ryecroft, the harassed toiler of so many a long year?

I dare not think of those I have left behind me, there in the ink-stained world. It would make me miserable, and to what purpose? Yet, having once looked that way, think of them I must. Oh, you heavy-laden, who at this hour sit down to the cursed travail of the pen; writing, not because there is something in your mind, in your heart, which must needs be uttered, but because the pen is the only tool you can handle, your only means of earning bread! Year after year the number of you is multiplied; you crowd the doors of publishers and editors, hustling, grappling, exchanging maledictions. Oh, sorry spectacle, grotesque and heart-breaking!

Innumerable are the men and women now writing for bread, who have not the least chance of finding in such work a permanent livelihood. They took to writing because they knew not what else to do, or because the literary calling tempted them by its independence and its dazzling prizes. They will hang on to the squalid profession, their earnings eked out by begging and borrowing, until it is too late for them to do anything else—and then? With a lifetime of dread experience behind me, I say that he who encourages any young man or woman to look for his living to "literature," commits no less than a crime. If my voice had any authority, I would cry this truth aloud wherever men could hear. Hateful as is the struggle for life in every form, this rough-and-tumble of the literary arena seems to me sordid and degrading beyond all others. Oh, your prices per thousand words! Oh, your paragraphings and your interviewings! And oh, the black despair that awaits those down-trodden in the fray.

Last midsummer I received a circular from a typewriting person, soliciting my custom; some one who had somehow got hold of my name, and fancied me to be still in purgatory. This person wrote: "If you should be in need of any extra assistance in the pressure of your Christmas work, I hope," etc.

How otherwise could one write if addressing a shopkeeper? "The pressure of your Christmas work"! Nay, I am too sick to laugh.

## XIX.

Some one, I see, is lifting up his sweet voice in praise of Conscription. It is only at long intervals that one reads this kind of thing in our reviews or newspapers, and I am happy in believing that most English people are affected by it even as I am, with the sickness of dread and of disgust. That the thing is impossible in England, who would venture to say? Every one who can think at all sees how slight are our safeguards against that barbaric force in man which the privileged races have so slowly and painfully brought into check. Democracy is full of menace to all the finer hopes of civilization, and the revival, in not unnatural companionship with it, of monarchic power based on militarism, makes the prospect dubious enough. There has but to arise some Lord of Slaughter, and the nations will be tearing at each other's throats. Let England be imperilled, and Englishmen will fight; in such extremity there is no choice. But what a dreary change must come upon our islanders if, without instant danger, they bend beneath the curse of universal soldiering! I like to think that they will guard the liberty of their manhood even beyond the point of prudence.

A lettered German, speaking to me once of his year of military service, told me that, had it lasted but a month or two longer, he must have sought release in suicide. I know very well that my own courage would not have borne me to the end of the twelvemonth; humiliation, resentment, loathing, would have goaded me to madness. At school we used to be "drilled" in the playground once a week; I have but to think of it, even after forty years, and there comes back upon me that tremor of passionate misery which, at the time, often made me ill. The senseless routine of mechanic exercise was in itself all but unendurable to me; I hated the standing in line, the thrusting-out of arms and legs at a signal, the thud of feet stamping in constrained unison. The loss of individuality seemed to me sheer disgrace.

And when, as often happened, the drill-sergeant rebuked me for some inefficiency as I stood in line, when he addressed me as "Number Seven!" I burned with shame and rage. I was no longer a human being; I had become part of a machine, and my name was "Number Seven." It used to astonish me when I had a neighbour who went through the drill with amusement, with zealous energy; I would gaze at the boy, and ask myself how it was possible that he and I should feel so differently. To be sure, nearly all my schoolfellows either enjoyed the thing, or at all events went through it with indifference; they made friends with the sergeant, and some were proud of walking with him "out of bounds." Left, right! Left, right! For my own part, I think I have never hated man as I hated that broad-shouldered, hard-visaged, brassy-voiced fellow. Every word he spoke to me, I felt as an insult. Seeing him in the distance, I have turned and fled, to escape the necessity of saluting, and, still more, a quiver of the nerves which affected me so painfully. If ever a man did me harm, it was he; harm physical and moral. In all seriousness I believe that something of the nervous instability from which I have suffered since boyhood is traceable to those accursed hours of drill, and I am very sure that I can date from the same wretched moments a fierceness of personal pride which has been one of my most troublesome characteristics. The disposition, of course, was there; it should have been modified, not exacerbated.

In younger manhood it would have flattered me to think that I alone on the school drill-ground had sensibility enough to suffer acutely. Now I had much rather feel assured that many of my schoolfellows were in the same mind of subdued revolt. Even of those who, boylike, enjoyed their drill, scarce one or two, I trust, would have welcomed in their prime of life the imposition of military servitude upon them and their countrymen. From a certain point of view, it would be better far that England should bleed under conquest than that she should be saved by eager, or careless, acceptance of Conscription. That view will not be held by the English people; but it would be a sorry thing for England if the day came when no one of those who love her harboured such a thought.

## XX.

It has occurred to me that one might define Art as: an expression, satisfying and abiding, of the zest of life. This is applicable to every form of Art devised by man, for, in his creative moment, whether he produce a great drama or carve a piece of foliage in wood, the artist is moved and inspired by supreme enjoyment of some aspect of the world about him; an enjoyment in itself keener than that experienced by another man, and intensified, prolonged, by the power—which comes to him we know not how—of recording in visible or audible form that emotion of rare vitality. Art, in some degree, is within the scope of every human being, were he but the ploughman who utters a few would-be melodious notes, the mere outcome of health and strength, in the field at sunrise; he sings, or tries to, prompted by an unusual gusto in being, and the rude stave is all his own. Another was he, who also at the plough, sang of the daisy, of the field-mouse, or shaped the rhythmic tale of Tam o' Shanter. Not only had life a zest for him incalculably stronger and subtler than that which stirs the soul of Hodge, but he uttered it in word and music such as go to the heart of mankind, and hold a magic power for ages.

For some years there has been a great deal of talk about Art in our country. It began, I suspect, when the veritable artistic impulse of the Victorian time had flagged, when the energy of a great time was all but exhausted. Principles always become a matter of vehement discussion when practice is at ebb. Not by taking thought does one become an artist, or grow even an inch in that direction—which is not at all the same as saying that he who *is* an artist cannot profit by conscious effort. Goethe (the example so often urged by imitators unlike him in every feature of humanity) took thought enough about his Faust; but what of those youthtime lyrics, not the least precious of his achievements, which were scribbled as fast as pen could go, thwartwise on the paper, because he could not stop to set it straight? Dare I pen, even for my own eyes, the venerable truth that an artist is born and not made? It seems not superfluous, in times which have heard disdainful criticism of Scott, on the ground that he had no artistic conscience, that he scribbled without a thought of style, that he never elaborated his scheme before beginning—as Flaubert, of course you know, invariably did. Why, after all, has one not heard that a certain William Shakespeare turned out his so-called works of art with something like criminal carelessness? Is it not a fact that a bungler named Cervantes was so little in earnest about his Art that, having in one chapter described the stealing of Sancho's donkey, he presently, in mere forgetfulness, shows us Sancho riding on Dapple, as if nothing had happened? Does not one Thackeray shamelessly avow on the last page of a grossly "subjective" novel that he had killed Lord Farintosh's mother at one page and brought her to life again at another? These sinners against Art are none the less among the world's supreme artists, for they *lived*, in a sense, in a degree, unintelligible to these critics of theirs, and their work is an expression, satisfying and abiding, of the zest of life.

Some one, no doubt, hit upon this definition of mine long ago. It doesn't matter; is it the less original with me? Not long since I should have fretted over the possibility, for my living depended on an avoidance of even seeming plagiarism. Now I am at one with Lord Foppington, and much disposed to take pleasure in the natural sprouts of my own wit—without troubling whether the same idea has occurred to others. Suppose me, in total ignorance of Euclid, to have discovered even the simplest of his geometrical demonstrations, shall I be crestfallen when some one draws attention to the book? These natural sprouts are, after all, the best products of our life; it is a mere accident that they may have no value in the world's market. One of my conscious efforts, in these days of freedom, is to live intellectually for myself. Formerly, when in reading I came upon anything that impressed or delighted me, down it went in my note-book, for "use." I could not read a striking verse, or sentence of prose, without thinking of it as an apt quotation in something I might write—one of the evil results of a literary life. Now that I strive to repel this habit of thought, I find myself asking: To what end, then, do I read and remember? Surely as foolish a question as ever man put to himself. You read for your own pleasure, for your solace and strengthening. Pleasure, then, purely selfish? Solace which endures for an hour, and strengthening for no combat? Ay, but I know, I know. With what heart should I live here in my cottage, waiting for life's end, were it not for those hours of seeming idle reading?

I think sometimes, how good it were had I some one by me to listen when I am tempted to read a passage aloud. Yes, but is there any mortal in the whole world upon whom I could invariably depend for sympathetic understanding?—nay, who would even generally be at one with me in my appreciation. Such harmony of intelligences is the rarest thing. All through life we long for it: the desire drives us, like a demon, into waste places; too often ends by plunging us into mud and morass. And, after all, we learn that the vision was illusory. To every man is it decreed: thou shalt live alone. Happy they who imagine that they have escaped the common lot; happy, whilst they imagine it. Those to whom no such happiness has ever been granted at least avoid the bitterest of disillusions. And is it not always good to face a truth, however discomfortable? The mind which renounces, once and for ever, a futile hope, has its compensation in ever-growing calm.

## XXI.

All about my garden to-day the birds are loud. To say that the air is filled with their song gives no idea of the ceaseless piping, whistling, trilling, which at moments rings to heaven in a triumphant unison, a wild accord. Now and then I notice one of the smaller songsters who seems to strain his throat in a madly joyous endeavour to out-carol all the rest. It is a chorus of praise such as none other of earth's children have the voice or the heart to utter. As I listen, I am carried away by its glorious rapture; my being melts in the tenderness of an impassioned joy; my eyes are dim with I know not what profound humility.

## XXII.

Were one to look at the literary journals only, and thereafter judge of the time, it would be easy to persuade oneself that civilization had indeed made great and solid progress, and that the world stood at a very hopeful stage of enlightenment. Week after week, I glance over these pages of crowded advertisement; I see a great many publishing-houses zealously active in putting forth every kind of book, new and old; I see names innumerable of workers in every branch of literature. Much that is announced declares itself at once of merely ephemeral import, or even of no import at all; but what masses of print which invite the attention of thoughtful or studious folk! To the multitude is offered a long succession of classic authors, in beautiful form, at a minimum cost; never were such treasures so cheaply and so gracefully set before all who can prize them. For the wealthy, there are volumes magnificent; lordly editions; works of art whereon have been lavished care and skill and expense incalculable. Here is exhibited the learning of the whole world and of all the ages; be a man's study what it will, in these columns, at one time or another he shall find that which appeals to him. Here are labours of the erudite, exercised on every subject that falls within learning's scope. Science brings forth its newest discoveries in earth and heaven; it speaks to the philosopher in his solitude, and to the crowd in the market-place. Curious pursuits of the mind at leisure are represented in publications numberless; trifles and oddities of intellectual savour; gatherings from every byway of human interest. For other moods there are the fabulists; to tell truth, they commonly hold the place of honour in these varied lists. Who shall count them? Who shall calculate their readers? Builders of verse are many; yet the observer will note that contemporary poets have but an inconspicuous standing in this index of the public taste. Travel, on the other hand, is largely represented; the general appetite for information about lands remote would appear to be only less keen than for the adventures of romance.

With these pages before one's eyes, must one not needs believe that things of the mind are a prime concern of our day? Who are the purchasers of these volumes ever pouring from the press? How is it possible for so great a commerce to flourish save as a consequence of national eagerness in this intellectual domain? Surely one must take for granted that throughout the land, in town and country, private libraries are growing apace; that by the people at large a great deal of time is devoted to reading; that literary ambition is one of the commonest spurs to effort?

It is the truth. All this may be said of contemporary England. But is it enough to set one's mind at ease regarding the outlook of our civilization?

Two things must be remembered. However considerable this literary traffic, regarded by itself, it is relatively of small extent. And, in the second place, literary activity is by no means an invariable proof of that mental attitude which marks the truly civilized man.

Lay aside the "literary organ," which appears once a week, and take up the newspaper, which comes forth every day, morning and evening. Here you get the true proportion of things. Read your daily news-sheet—that which costs threepence or that which costs a halfpenny—and muse upon the impression it leaves. It may be that a few books are "noticed"; granting that the "notice" is in any way noticeable, compare the space it occupies with that devoted to the material interests of life: you have a gauge of the real importance of intellectual endeavour to the people at large. No, the public which reads, in any sense of the word worth considering, is very, very small; the public which would feel no lack if all book-printing ceased to-morrow, is enormous. These announcements of learned works which strike one as so encouraging, are addressed, as a matter of fact, to a few thousand persons, scattered all over the English-speaking world. Many of the most valuable books slowly achieve the sale of a few hundred copies. Gather from all the ends of the British Empire the men and women who purchase grave literature as a matter of course, who habitually seek it in public libraries, in short who regard it as a necessity of life, and I am much mistaken if they could not comfortably assemble in the Albert Hall.

But even granting this, is it not an obvious fact that our age tends to the civilized habit of mind, as displayed in a love for intellectual things? Was there ever a time which saw the literature of knowledge and of the emotions so widely distributed? Does not the minority of the truly intelligent exercise a vast and profound influence? Does it not in truth lead the way, however slowly and irregularly the multitude may follow?

I should like to believe it. When gloomy evidence is thrust upon me, I often say to myself: Think of the frequency of the reasonable man; think of him everywhere labouring to spread the light; how is it possible that such efforts should be overborne by forces of blind brutality, now that the human race has got so far?—Yes, yes; but this mortal whom I caress as reasonable, as enlightened and enlightening, this author, investigator, lecturer, or studious gentleman, to whose coat-tails I cling, does he always represent justice and peace, sweetness of manners, purity of life—all the things which makes for true civilization? Here is a fallacy of bookish thought. Experience offers proof on every hand that vigorous mental life may be but one side of a personality, of which the other is moral barbarism. A man may be a fine archaeologist, and yet have no sympathy with human ideals. The historian, the biographer, even the poet, may be a money-market gambler, a social toady, a clamorous Chauvinist, or an unscrupulous wire-puller. As for "leaders of science," what optimist will dare to proclaim them on the side of the gentle virtues? And if one must needs think in this way of those who stand forth, professed instructors and inspirers, what of those who merely listen? The reading-public—oh, the reading-public! Hardly will a prudent statistician venture to declare that one in every score of those who actually read sterling books do so with comprehension of their author. These dainty series of noble and delightful works, which have so seemingly wide an acceptance, think you they vouch for true appreciation in all who buy them? Remember those who purchase to follow the fashion, to impose upon their neighbour, or even to flatter themselves; think of those who wish to make cheap presents, and those who are merely pleased by the outer aspect of the volume. Above all, bear in mind that busy throng whose zeal is according neither to knowledge nor to conviction, the host of the half-educated, characteristic and peril of our time. They, indeed, purchase and purchase largely. Heaven forbid that I should not recognize the few among them whose bent of brain and of conscience justifies their fervour; to such—the ten in ten thousand—be all aid and brotherly solace! But the glib many, the perky mispronouncers of titles and of authors' names, the twanging murderers of rhythm, the maulers of the uncut edge at sixpence extra, the ready-reckoners of bibliopolic discount—am I to see in these a witness of my hope for the century to come?

I am told that their semi-education will be integrated. We are in a transition stage, between the bad old time when only a few had academic privileges, and that happy future which will see all men liberally instructed. Unfortunately for this argument, education is a thing of which only the few are capable; teach as you will, only a small percentage will profit by your most zealous energy. On an ungenerous soil it is vain to look for rich crops. Your average mortal will be your average mortal still: and if he grow conscious of power, if he becomes vocal and self-assertive, if he get into his hands all the material resources of the country, why, you have a state of things such as at present looms menacingly before every Englishman blessed—or cursed—with an unpopular spirit.

## XXIII.

Every morning when I awake, I thank heaven for silence. This is my orison. I remember the London days when sleep was broken by clash and clang, by roar and shriek, and when my first sense on returning to consciousness was hatred of the life about me. Noises of wood and metal, clattering of wheels, banging of implements, jangling of bells—all such things are bad enough, but worse still is the clamorous human voice. Nothing on earth is more irritating to me than a bellow or scream of idiot mirth, nothing more hateful than a shout or yell of brutal anger. Were it possible, I would never again hear the utterance of a human tongue, save from those few who are dear to me.

Here, wake at what hour I may, early or late, I lie amid gracious stillness. Perchance a horse's hoof rings rhythmically upon the road; perhaps a dog barks from a neighbour farm; it may be that there comes the far, soft murmur of a train from the other side of Exe; but these are almost the only sounds that could force themselves upon my ear. A voice, at any time of the day, is the rarest thing.

But there is the rustle of branches in the morning breeze; there is the music of a sunny shower against the window; there is the matin song of birds. Several times lately I have lain wakeful when there sounded the first note of the earliest lark; it makes me almost glad of my restless nights. The only trouble that touches me in these moments is the thought of my long life wasted amid the senseless noises of man's world. Year after year this spot has known the same tranquillity; with ever so little of good fortune, with ever so little wisdom, beyond what was granted me, I might have blessed my manhood with calm, might have made for myself in later life a long retrospect of bowered peace. As it is, I enjoy with something of sadness, remembering that this melodious silence is but the prelude of that deeper stillness which waits to enfold us all.

## XXIV.

Morning after morning, of late, I have taken my walk in the same direction, my purpose being to look at a plantation of young larches. There is no lovelier colour on earth than that in which they are now clad; it seems to refresh as well as gladden my eyes, and its influence sinks deep into my heart. Too soon it will change; already I think the first radiant verdure has begun to pass into summer's soberness. The larch has its moment of unmatched beauty—and well for him whose chance permits him to enjoy it, spring after spring.

Could anything be more wonderful than the fact that here am I, day by day, not only at leisure to walk forth and gaze at the larches, but blessed with the tranquillity of mind needful for such enjoyment? On any morning of spring sunshine, how many mortals find themselves so much at peace that they are able to give themselves wholly to delight in the glory of heaven and of earth? Is it the case with one man in every fifty thousand? Consider what extraordinary kindness of fate must tend upon one, that not a care, not a preoccupation, should interfere with his contemplative thought for five or six days successively! So rooted in the human mind (and so reasonably rooted) is the belief in an Envious Power, that I ask myself whether I shall not have to pay, by some disaster, for this period of sacred calm. For a week or so I have been one of a small number, chosen out of the whole human race by fate's supreme benediction. It may be that this comes to every one in turn; to most, it can only be once in a lifetime, and so briefly. That my own lot seems so much better than that of ordinary men, sometimes makes me fearful.

## XXV.

Walking in a favourite lane to-day, I found it covered with shed blossoms of the hawthorn. Creamy white, fragrant even in ruin, lay scattered the glory of the May. It told me that spring is over.

Have I enjoyed it as I should? Since the day that brought me freedom, four times have I seen the year's new birth, and always, as the violet yielded to the rose, I have known a fear that I had not sufficiently prized this boon of heaven whilst it was with me. Many hours I have spent shut up among my books, when I might have been in the meadows. Was the gain equivalent? Doubtfully, diffidently, I hearken what the mind can plead.

I recall my moments of delight, the recognition of each flower that unfolded, the surprise of budding branches clothed in a night with green. The first snowy gleam upon the blackthorn did not escape me. By its familiar bank, I watched for the earliest primrose, and in its copse I found the anemone. Meadows shining with buttercups, hollows sunned with the marsh marigold held me long at gaze. I saw the sallow glistening with its cones of silvery fur, and splendid with dust of gold. These common things touch me with more of admiration and of wonder each time I behold them. They are once more gone. As I turn to summer, a misgiving mingles with my joy.

# SUMMER

## I.

To-day, as I was reading in the garden, a waft of summer perfume—some hidden link of association in what I read—I know not what it may have been—took me back to school-boy holidays; I recovered with strange intensity that lightsome mood of long release from tasks, of going away to the seaside, which is one of childhood's blessings. I was in the train; no rushing express, such as bears you great distances; the sober train which goes to no place of importance, which lets you see the white steam of the engine float and fall upon a meadow ere you pass. Thanks to a good and wise father, we youngsters saw nothing of seaside places where crowds assemble; I am speaking, too, of a time more than forty years ago, when it was still possible to find on the coasts of northern England, east or west, spots known only to those who loved the shore for its beauty and its solitude. At every station the train stopped; little stations, decked with beds of flowers, smelling warm in the sunshine where country-folk got in with baskets, and talked in an unfamiliar dialect, an English which to us sounded almost like a foreign tongue. Then the first glimpse of the sea; the excitement of noting whether tide was high or low—stretches of sand and weedy pools, or halcyon wavelets frothing at their furthest reach, under the sea-banks starred with convolvulus. Of a sudden, *our* station!

Ah, that taste of the brine on a child's lips! Nowadays, I can take holiday when I will, and go whithersoever it pleases me; but that salt kiss of the sea air I shall never know again. My senses are dulled; I cannot get so near to Nature; I have a sorry dread of her clouds, her winds, and must walk with tedious circumspection where once I ran and leapt exultingly. Were it possible, but for one half-hour, to plunge and bask in the sunny surf, to roll on the silvery sand-hills, to leap from rock to rock on shining sea-ferns, laughing if I slipped into the shallows among starfish and anemones! I am much older in body than in mind; I can but look at what I once enjoyed.

## II.

I have been spending a week in Somerset. The right June weather put me in the mind for rambling, and my thoughts turned to the Severn Sea. I went to Glastonbury and Wells, and on to Cheddar, and so to the shore of the Channel at Clevedon, remembering my holiday of fifteen years ago, and too often losing myself in a contrast of the man I was then and what I am now. Beautiful beyond all words of description that nook of oldest England; but that I feared the moist and misty winter climate, I should have chosen some spot below the Mendips for my home and resting-place. Unspeakable the charm to my ear of those old names; exquisite the quiet of those little towns, lost amid tilth and pasture, untouched as yet by the fury of modern life, their ancient sanctuaries guarded, as it were, by noble trees and hedges overrun with flowers. In all England there is no sweeter and more varied prospect than that from the hill of the Holy Thorn at Glastonbury; in all England there is no lovelier musing place than the leafy walk beside the Palace Moat at Wells. As I think of the golden hours I spent there, a passion to which I can give no name takes hold upon me; my heart trembles with an indefinable ecstasy.

There was a time of my life when I was consumed with a desire for foreign travel; an impatience of everything familiar fretted me through all the changing year. If I had not at length found the opportunity to escape, if I had not seen the landscapes for which my soul longed, I think I must have moped to death. Few men, assuredly, have enjoyed such wanderings more than I, and few men revive them in memory with a richer delight or deeper longing. But—whatever temptation comes to me in mellow autumn, when I think of the grape and of the olive—I do not believe I shall ever again cross the sea. What remains to me of life and of energy is far too little for the enjoyment of all I know, and all I wish to know, of this dear island.

As a child I used to sleep in a room hung round with prints after English landscape painters—those steel engravings so common half a century ago, which bore the legend, "From the picture in the Vernon Gallery." Far more than I knew at the time, these pictures impressed me; I gazed and gazed at them, with that fixed attention of a child which is half curiosity, half reverie, till every line of them was fixed in my mind; at this moment I see the black-and-white landscapes as if they were hanging on the wall before me, and I have often thought that this early training of the imagination—for such it was—has much to do with the passionate love of rural scenery which lurked within me even when I did not recognize it, and which now for many a year has been one of the emotions directing my life. Perhaps, too, that early memory explains why I love a good black-and-white print even more than a good painting. And—to draw yet another inference—here may be a reason for the fact that, through my youth and early manhood, I found more pleasure in Nature as represented by art than in Nature herself. Even during that strange time when hardships and passions held me captive far from any glimpse of the flowering earth, I could be moved, and moved deeply, by a picture of the simplest rustic scene. At rare moments, when a happy chance led me into the National Gallery, I used to stand long before such pictures as "The Valley Farm," "The Cornfield," "Mousehold Heath." In the murk confusion of my heart these visions of the world of peace and beauty from which I was excluded—to which, indeed, I hardly ever gave a thought—touched me to deep emotion. But it did not need—nor does it now—the magic of a master to awake that mood in me. Let me but come upon the poorest little woodcut, the cheapest "process" illustration, representing a thatched cottage, a lane, a field, and I hear that music begin to murmur. It is a passion—Heaven be thanked—that grows with my advancing years. The last thought of my brain as I lie dying will be that of sunshine upon an English meadow.

### III.

Sitting in my garden amid the evening scent of roses, I have read through Walton's *Life of Hooker*; could any place and time have been more appropriate? Almost within sight is the tower of Heavitree church—Heavitree, which was Hooker's birthplace. In other parts of England he must often have thought of these meadows falling to the green valley of the Exe, and of the sun setting behind the pines of Haldon. Hooker loved the country. Delightful to me, and infinitely touching, is that request of his to be transferred from London to a rural living—"where I can see God's blessing spring out of the earth." And that glimpse of him where he was found tending sheep, with a Horace in his hand. It was in rural solitudes that he conceived the rhythm of mighty prose. What music of the spheres sang to that poor, vixen-haunted, pimply-faced man!

The last few pages I read by the light of the full moon, that of afterglow having till then sufficed me. Oh, why has it not been granted me in all my long years of pen-labour to write something small and perfect, even as one of these lives of honest Izaak! Here is literature, look you—not "literary work." Let me be thankful that I have the mind to enjoy it; not only to understand, but to savour, its great goodness.

### IV.

It is Sunday morning, and above earth's beauty shines the purest, softest sky this summer has yet gladdened us withal. My window is thrown open; I see the sunny gleam upon garden leaves and flowers; I hear the birds whose wont it is to sing to me; ever and anon the martins that have their home beneath my eaves sweep past in silence. Church bells have begun to chime; I know the music of their voices, near and far.

There was a time when it delighted me to flash my satire on the English Sunday; I could see nothing but antiquated foolishness and modern hypocrisy in this weekly pause from labour and from bustle. Now I prize it as an inestimable boon, and dread every encroachment upon its restful stillness. Scoff as I might at "Sabbatarianism," was I not always glad when Sunday came? The bells of London churches and chapels are not soothing to the ear, but when I remember their sound—even that of the most aggressively pharisaic conventicle, with its one dire clapper—I find it associated with a sense of repose, of liberty. This day of the seven I granted to my better genius; work was put aside, and, when Heaven permitted, trouble forgotten.

When out of England I have always missed this Sunday quietude, this difference from ordinary days which seems to affect the very atmosphere. It is not enough that people should go to church, that shops should be closed and workyards silent; these holiday notes do not make a Sunday. Think as one may of its significance, our Day of Rest has a peculiar sanctity, felt, I imagine, in a more or less vague way, even by those who wish to see the village lads at cricket and theatres open in the town. The idea is surely as good a one as ever came to heavy-laden mortals; let one whole day in every week be removed from the common life of the world, lifted above common pleasures as above common cares. With all the abuses of fanaticism, this thought remained rich in blessings; Sunday has always brought large good to the generality, and to a chosen number has been the very life of the soul, however heretically some of them understood the words. If its ancient use perish from among us, so much the worse for our country. And perish no doubt it will; only here in rustic solitude can one forget the changes that have already made the day less sacred to multitudes. With it will vanish that habit of periodic calm, which, even when it has become so largely void of conscious meaning, is, one may safely say, the best spiritual boon ever bestowed upon a people. The most difficult of all things to attain, the most difficult of all to preserve, the supreme benediction of the noblest mind, this calm was once breathed over the whole land as often as sounded the last stroke of weekly toil; on Saturday at even began the quiet and the solace. With the decline of old faith, Sunday cannot but lose its sanction, and no loss among the innumerable that we are suffering will work so effectually for popular vulgarization. What hope is there of guarding the moral beauty of the day when the authority which set it apart is no longer recognized?—Imagine a bank-holiday once a week!

## V.

On Sunday I come down later than usual; I make a change of dress, for it is fitting that the day of spiritual rest should lay aside the livery of the laborious week. For me, indeed, there is no labour at any time, but nevertheless does Sunday bring me repose. I share in the common tranquillity; my thought escapes the workaday world more completely than on other days.

It is not easy to see how this house of mine can make to itself a Sunday quiet, for at all times it is well-nigh soundless; yet I find a difference. My housekeeper comes into the room with her Sunday smile; she is happier for the day, and the sight of her happiness gives me pleasure. She speaks, if possible, in a softer voice; she wears a garment which reminds me that there is only the lightest and cleanest housework to be done. She will go to church, morning and evening, and I know that she is better for it. During her absence I sometimes look into rooms which on other days I never enter; it is merely to gladden my eyes with the shining cleanliness, the perfect order, I am sure to find in the good woman's domain. But for that spotless and sweet-smelling kitchen, what would it avail me to range my books and hang my pictures? All the tranquillity of my life depends upon the honest care of this woman who lives and works unseen. And I am sure that the money I pay her is the least part of her reward. She is such an old-fashioned person that the mere discharge of what she deems a duty is in itself an end to her, and the work of her hands in itself a satisfaction, a pride.

When a child, I was permitted to handle on Sunday certain books which could not be exposed to the more careless usage of common days; volumes finely illustrated, or the more handsome editions of familiar authors, or works which, merely by their bulk, demanded special care. Happily, these books were all of the higher rank in literature, and so there came to be established in my mind an association between the day of rest and names which are the greatest in verse and prose. Through my life this habit has remained with me; I have always wished to spend some part of the Sunday quiet with books which, at most times, it is fatally easy to leave aside, one's very knowledge and love of them serving as an excuse for their neglect in favour of print which has the attraction of newness. Homer and Virgil, Milton and Shakespeare; not many Sundays have gone by without my opening one or other of these. Not many Sundays? Nay, that is to exaggerate, as one has the habit of doing. Let me say rather that, on many a rest-day I have found mind and opportunity for such reading. Nowadays mind and opportunity fail me never. I may take down my Homer or my Shakespeare when I choose, but it is still on Sunday that I feel it most becoming to seek the privilege of their companionship. For these great ones, crowned with immortality, do not respond to him who approaches them as though hurried by temporal care. There befits the garment of solemn leisure, the thought attuned to peace. I open the volume somewhat formally; is it not sacred, if the word have any meaning at all? And, as I read, no interruption can befall me. The note of a linnet, the humming of a bee, these are the sounds about my sanctuary. The page scarce rustles as it turns.

# VI.

Of how many dwellings can it be said that no word of anger is ever heard beneath its roof, and that no unkindly feeling ever exists between the inmates? Most men's experience would seem to justify them in declaring that, throughout the inhabited world, no such house exists. I, knowing at all events of one, admit the possibility that there may be more; yet I feel that it is to hazard a conjecture; I cannot point with certainty to any other instance, nor in all my secular life (I speak as one who has quitted the world) could I have named a single example.

It is so difficult for human beings to live together; nay, it is so difficult for them to associate, however transitorily, and even under the most favourable conditions, without some shadow of mutual offence. Consider the differences of task and of habit, the conflict of prejudices, the divergence of opinions (though that is probably the same thing), which quickly reveal themselves between any two persons brought into more than casual contact, and think how much self-subdual is implicit whenever, for more than an hour or two, they co-exist in seeming harmony. Man is not made for peaceful intercourse with his fellows; he is by nature self-assertive, commonly aggressive, always critical in a more or less hostile spirit of any characteristic which seems strange to him. That he is capable of profound affections merely modifies here and there his natural contentiousness, and subdues its expression. Even love, in the largest and purest sense of the word, is no safeguard against perilous irritation and sensibilities inborn. And what were the durability of love without the powerful alliance of habit?

Suppose yourself endowed with such power of hearing that all the talk going on at any moment beneath the domestic roofs of any town became clearly audible to you; the dominant note would be that of moods, tempers, opinions at jar. Who but the most amiable dreamer can doubt it? This, mind you, is not the same thing as saying that angry emotion is the ruling force in human life; the facts of our civilization prove the contrary. Just because, and only because, the natural spirit of conflict finds such frequent scope, does human society hold together, and, on the whole, present a pacific aspect. In the course of ages (one would like to know how many) man has attained a remarkable degree of self-control; dire experience has forced upon him the necessity of compromise, and habit has inclined him (the individual) to prefer a quiet, orderly life. But by instinct he is still a quarrelsome creature, and he gives vent to the impulse as far as it is compatible with his reasoned interests—often, to be sure, without regard for that limit. The average man or woman is always at open discord with some one; the great majority could not live without oft-recurrent squabble. Speak in confidence with any one you like, and get him to tell you how many cases of coldness, alienation, or downright enmity, between friends and kinsfolk, his memory registers; the number will be considerable, and what a vastly greater number of everyday "misunderstandings" may be thence inferred! Verbal contention is, of course, commoner among the poor and the vulgar than in the class of well-bred people living at their ease, but I doubt whether the lower ranks of society find personal association much more difficult than the refined minority above them. High cultivation may help to self-command, but it multiplies the chances of irritative contact. In mansion, as in hovel, the strain of life is perpetually felt—between the married, between parents and children, between relatives of every degree, between employers and employed. They debate, they dispute, they wrangle, they explode—then nerves are relieved, and they are ready to begin over again. Quit the home and quarrelling is less obvious, but it goes on all about one. What proportion of the letters delivered any morning would be found to be written in displeasure, in petulance, in wrath? The postbag shrieks insults or bursts with suppressed malice. Is it not wonderful—nay, is it not the marvel of marvels—that human life has reached such a high point of public and private organization?

And gentle idealists utter their indignant wonder at the continuance of war! Why, it passes the wit of man to explain how it is that nations are ever at peace! For, if only by the rarest good fortune do individuals associate harmoniously, there would seem to be much less likelihood of mutual understanding and good-will between the peoples of alien lands. As a matter of fact, no two nations are ever friendly, in the sense of truly liking each other; with the reciprocal criticism of countries there always mingles a sentiment of animosity. The original meaning of *hostis* is merely stranger, and a stranger who is likewise a foreigner will only by curious exception fail to stir antipathy in the average human being. Add to this that a great number of persons in every country find their delight and their business in exasperating international disrelish, and with what vestige of common sense can one feel surprise that war is ceaselessly talked of, often enough declared. In days gone by, distance and rarity of communication assured peace between many realms. Now that every country is in proximity to every other, what need is there to elaborate explanations of the distrust, the fear, the hatred, which are a perpetual theme of journalists and statesmen? By approximation, all countries have entered the sphere of natural quarrel. That they find plenty of things to quarrel about is no cause for astonishment. A hundred years hence there will be some possibility of perceiving whether international relations are likely to obey the law which has acted with such beneficence in the life of each civilized people; whether this country and that will be content to ease their tempers with bloodless squabbling, subduing the more violent promptings for the common good. Yet I suspect that a century is a very short time to allow for even justifiable

surmise of such an outcome. If by any chance newspapers ceased to exist .
. .

Talk of war, and one gets involved in such utopian musings!

## VII.

I have been reading one of those prognostic articles on international
politics which every now and then appear in the reviews. Why I should so
waste my time it would be hard to say; I suppose the fascination of disgust
and fear gets the better of me in a moment's idleness. This writer, who is
horribly perspicacious and vigorous, demonstrates the certainty of a great
European war, and regards it with the peculiar satisfaction excited by such
things in a certain order of mind. His phrases about "dire calamity" and so
on mean nothing; the whole tenor of his writing proves that he represents,
and consciously, one of the forces which go to bring war about; his part in
the business is a fluent irresponsibility, which casts scorn on all who reluct
at the "inevitable." Persistent prophecy is a familiar way of assuring the
event.

But I will read no more such writing. This resolution I make and will keep.
Why set my nerves quivering with rage, and spoil the calm of a whole day,
when no good of any sort can come of it? What is it to me if nations fall a-
slaughtering each other? Let the fools go to it! Why should they not please
themselves? Peace, after all, is the aspiration of the few; so it always; was,
and ever will be. But have done with the nauseous cant about "dire
calamity." The leaders and the multitude hold no such view; either they see
in war a direct and tangible profit, or they are driven to it, with heads down,
by the brute that is in them. Let them rend and be rent; let them paddle in
blood and viscera till—if that would ever happen—their stomachs turn.
Let them blast the cornfield and the orchard, fire the home. For all that,
there will yet be found some silent few, who go their way amid the still
meadows, who bend to the flower and watch the sunset; and these alone
are worth a thought.

## VIII.

In this hot weather I like to walk at times amid the full glow of the sun.
Our island sun is never hot beyond endurance, and there is a magnificence
in the triumph of high summer which exalts one's mind. Among streets it
is hard to bear, yet even there, for those who have eyes to see it, the
splendour of the sky lends beauty to things in themselves mean or hideous.
I remember an August bank-holiday, when, having for some reason to walk
all across London, I unexpectedly found myself enjoying the strange
desertion of great streets, and from that passed to surprise in the sense of
something beautiful, a charm in the vulgar vista, in the dull architecture,

which I had never known. Deep and clear-marked shadows, such as one only sees on a few days of summer, are in themselves very impressive, and become more so when they fall upon highways devoid of folk. I remember observing, as something new, the shape of familiar edifices, of spires, monuments. And when at length I sat down, somewhere on the Embankment, it was rather to gaze at leisure than to rest, for I felt no weariness, and the sun, still pouring upon me its noontide radiance, seemed to fill my veins with life.

That sense I shall never know again. For me Nature has comforts, raptures, but no more invigoration. The sun keeps me alive, but cannot, as in the old days, renew my being. I would fain learn to enjoy without reflecting.

My walk in the golden hours leads me to a great horse-chestnut, whose root offers a convenient seat in the shadow of its foliage. At that resting-place I have no wide view before me, but what I see is enough—a corner of waste land, over-flowered with poppies and charlock, on the edge of a field of corn. The brilliant red and yellow harmonize with the glory of the day. Near by, too, is a hedge covered with great white blooms of the bindweed. My eyes do not soon grow weary.

A little plant of which I am very fond is the rest-harrow. When the sun is hot upon it, the flower gives forth a strangely aromatic scent, very delightful to me. I know the cause of this peculiar pleasure. The rest-harrow sometimes grows in sandy ground above the seashore. In my childhood I have many a time lain in such a spot under the glowing sky, and, though I scarce thought of it, perceived the odour of the little rose-pink flower when it touched my face. Now I have but to smell it, and those hours come back again. I see the shore of Cumberland, running north to St. Bee's Head; on the sea horizon a faint shape which is the Isle of Man; inland, the mountains, which for me at that time guarded a region of unknown wonder. Ah, how long ago!

## IX.

I read much less than I used to do; I think much more. Yet what is the use of thought which can no longer serve to direct life? Better, perhaps, to read and read incessantly, losing one's futile self in the activity of other minds.

This summer I have taken up no new book, but have renewed my acquaintance with several old ones which I had not opened for many a year. One or two have been books such as mature men rarely read at all— books which it is one's habit to "take as read"; to presume sufficiently known to speak of, but never to open. Thus, one day my hand fell upon the *Anabasis*, the little Oxford edition which I used at school, with its boyish sign-manual on the fly-leaf, its blots and underlinings and marginal scrawls. To my shame I possess no other edition; yet this is a book one would like to have in beautiful form. I opened it, I began to read—a ghost of boyhood stirring in my heart—and from chapter to chapter was led on, until after a few days I had read the whole.

I am glad this happened in the summer-time, I like to link childhood with these latter days, and no better way could I have found than this return to a school-book, which, even as a school-book, was my great delight.

By some trick of memory I always associate school-boy work on the classics with a sense of warm and sunny days; rain and gloom and a chilly atmosphere must have been far the more frequent conditions, but these things are forgotten. My old Liddell and Scott still serves me, and if, in opening it, I bend close enough to catch the *scent* of the leaves, I am back again at that day of boyhood (noted on the fly-leaf by the hand of one long dead) when the book was new and I used it for the first time. It was a day of summer, and perhaps there fell upon the unfamiliar page, viewed with childish tremor, half apprehension and half delight, a mellow sunshine, which was to linger for ever in my mind.

But I am thinking of the *Anabasis*. Were this the sole book existing in Greek, it would be abundantly worth while to learn the language in order to read it. The *Anabasis* is an admirable work of art, unique in its combination of concise and rapid narrative with colour and picturesqueness. Herodotus wrote a prose epic, in which the author's personality is ever before us. Xenophon, with curiosity and love of adventure which mark him of the same race, but self-forgetful in the pursuit of a new artistic virtue, created the historical romance. What a world of wonders in this little book, all aglow with ambitions and conflicts, with marvels of strange lands; full of perils and rescues, fresh with the air of mountain and of sea! Think of it for a moment by the side of Caesar's Commentaries; not to compare things incomparable, but in order to appreciate the perfect art which shines through Xenophon's mastery of language, his brevity achieving a result so different from that of the like characteristic in the Roman writer. Caesar's conciseness comes of strength and pride; Xenophon's, of a vivid imagination. Many a single line of the *Anabasis* presents a picture which deeply stirs the emotions. A good instance occurs in the fourth book, where a delightful passage of unsurpassable narrative tells how the Greeks rewarded and dismissed a guide who had led them through dangerous country. The man himself was in peril of his life; laden with valuable things which the soldiers had given him in their gratitude, he turned to make his way through the hostile region. Ἐπει εσπερα εγενετο, ωχετο της νυκτος. "When evening came he took leave of us, and went his way by night." To my mind, words of wonderful suggestiveness. You see the wild, eastern landscape, upon which the sun has set. There are the Hellenes, safe for the moment on their long march, and there the mountain tribesman, the serviceable barbarian, going away, alone, with his tempting guerdon, into the hazards of the darkness.

Also in the fourth book, another picture moves one in another way. Among the Carduchian Hills two men were seized, and information was sought from them about the track to be followed. "One of them would say nothing, and kept silence in spite of every threat; so, in the presence of his companion, he was slain. Thereupon that other made known the man's reason for refusing to point out the way; in the direction the Greeks must take there dwelt a daughter of his, who was married."

It would not be easy to express more pathos than is conveyed in these few words. Xenophon himself, one may be sure, did not feel it quite as we do, but he preserved the incident for its own sake, and there, in a line or two, shines something of human love and sacrifice, significant for all time.

## X.

I sometimes think I will go and spend the sunny half of a twelvemonth in wandering about the British Isles. There is so much of beauty and interest that I have not seen, and I grudge to close my eyes on this beloved home of ours, leaving any corner of it unvisited. Often I wander in fancy over all the parts I know, and grow restless with desire at familiar names which bring no picture to memory. My array of county guide-books (they have always been irresistible to me on the stalls) sets me roaming; the only dull pages in them are those that treat of manufacturing towns. Yet I shall never start on that pilgrimage. I am too old, too fixed in habits. I dislike the railway; I dislike hotels. I should grow homesick for my library, my garden, the view from my windows. And then—I have such a fear of dying anywhere but under my own roof.

As a rule, it is better to revisit only in imagination the places which have greatly charmed us, or which, in the retrospect, seem to have done so. Seem to have charmed us, I say; for the memory we form, after a certain lapse of time, of places where we lingered, often bears but a faint resemblance to the impression received at the time; what in truth may have been very moderate enjoyment, or enjoyment greatly disturbed by inner or outer circumstances, shows in the distance as a keen delight, or as deep, still happiness. On the other hand, if memory creates no illusion, and the name of a certain place is associated with one of the golden moments of life, it were rash to hope that another visit would repeat the experience of a bygone day. For it was not merely the sights that one beheld which were the cause of joy and peace; however lovely the spot, however gracious the sky, these things external would not have availed, but for contributory movements of mind and heart and blood, the essentials of the man as then he was.

Whilst I was reading this afternoon my thoughts strayed, and I found myself recalling a hillside in Suffolk, where, after a long walk I rested drowsily one midsummer day twenty years ago. A great longing seized me; I was tempted to set off at once, and find again that spot under the high elm trees, where, as I smoked a delicious pipe, I heard about me the crack, crack, crack of broom-pods bursting in the glorious heat of the noontide sun. Had I acted upon the impulse, what chance was there of my enjoying such another hour as that which my memory cherished? No, no; it is not the *place* that I remember; it is the time of life, the circumstances, the mood, which at that moment fell so happily together. Can I dream that a pipe smoked on that same hillside, under the same glowing sky, would taste as it then did, or bring me the same solace? Would the turf be so soft beneath me? Would the great elm-branches temper so delightfully the noontide rays beating upon them? And, when the hour of rest was over, should I spring to my feet as then I did, eager to put forth my strength again? No, no; what I remember is just one moment of my earlier life, linked by accident with that picture of the Suffolk landscape. The place no longer exists; it never existed save for me. For it is the mind which creates the world about us, and, even though we stand side by side in the same meadow, my eyes will never see what is beheld by yours, my heart will never stir to the emotions with which yours is touched.

## XI.

I awoke a little after four o'clock. There was sunlight upon the blind, that pure gold of the earliest beam which always makes me think of Dante's angels. I had slept unusually well, without a dream, and felt the blessing of rest through all my frame; my head was clear, my pulse beat temperately. And, when I had lain thus for a few minutes, asking myself what book I should reach from the shelf that hangs near my pillow, there came upon me a desire to rise and go forth into the early morning. On the moment I bestirred myself. The drawing up of the blind, the opening of the window, only increased my zeal, and I was soon in the garden, then out in the road, walking light-heartedly I cared not whither.

How long is it since I went forth at the hour of summer sunrise? It is one of the greatest pleasures, physical and mental, that any man in moderate health can grant himself; yet hardly once in a year do mood and circumstance combine to put it within one's reach. The habit of lying in bed hours after broad daylight is strange enough, if one thinks of it; a habit entirely evil; one of the most foolish changes made by modern system in the healthier life of the old time. But that my energies are not equal to such great innovation, I would begin going to bed at sunset and rising with the beam of day; ten to one, it would vastly improve my health, and undoubtedly it would add to the pleasures of my existence.

When travelling, I have now and then watched the sunrise, and always with an exultation unlike anything produced in me by other aspects of nature. I remember daybreak on the Mediterranean; the shapes of islands growing in hue after hue of tenderest light, until they floated amid a sea of glory. And among the mountains—that crowning height, one moment a cold pallor, the next soft-glowing under the touch of the rosy-fingered goddess. These are the things I shall never see again; things, indeed, so perfect in memory that I should dread to blur them by a newer experience. My senses are so much duller; they do not show me what once they did.

How far away is that school-boy time, when I found a pleasure in getting up and escaping from the dormitory whilst all the others were still asleep. My purpose was innocent enough; I got up early only to do my lessons. I can see the long school-room, lighted by the early sun; I can smell the school-room odour—a blend of books and slates and wall-maps and I know not what. It was a mental peculiarity of mine that at five o'clock in the morning I could apply myself with gusto to mathematics, a subject loathsome to me at any other time of the day. Opening the book at some section which was wont to scare me, I used to say to myself: "Come now, I'm going to tackle this this morning! If other boys can understand it, why shouldn't I?" And in a measure I succeeded. In a measure only; there was always a limit at which my powers failed me, strive as I would.

In my garret-days it was seldom that I rose early: with the exception of one year—or the greater part of a twelvemonth—during which I was regularly up at half-past five for a special reason. I had undertaken to "coach" a man for the London matriculation; he was in business, and the only time he could conveniently give to his studies was before breakfast. I, just then, had my lodgings near Hampstead Road; my pupil lived at Knightsbridge; I engaged to be with him every morning at half-past six, and the walk, at a brisk pace, took me just about an hour. At that time I saw no severity in the arrangement, and I was delighted to earn the modest fee which enabled me to write all day long without fear of hunger; but one inconvenience attached to it. I had no watch, and my only means of knowing the time was to hear the striking of a clock in the neighbourhood. As a rule, I awoke just when I should have done; the clock struck five, and up I sprang. But occasionally—and this when the mornings had grown dark—my punctual habit failed me; I would hear the clock chime some fraction of the hour, and could not know whether I had awoke too soon or slept too long. The horror of unpunctuality, which has always been a craze with me, made it impossible to lie waiting; more than once I dressed and went out into the street to discover as best I could what time it was, and one such expedition, I well remember, took place between two and three o'clock on a morning of foggy rain.

It happened now and then that, on reaching the house at Knightsbridge, I was informed that Mr. --- felt too tired to rise. This concerned me little, for it meant no deduction of fee; I had the two hours' walk, and was all the better for it. Then the appetite with which I sat down to breakfast, whether I had done my coaching or not! Bread and butter and coffee—such coffee!—made the meal, and I ate like a navvy. I was in magnificent spirits. All the way home I had been thinking of my day's work, and the morning brain, clarified and whipped to vigour by that brisk exercise, by that wholesome hunger, wrought its best. The last mouthful swallowed, I was seated at my writing-table; aye, and there I sat for seven or eight hours, with a short munching interval, working as only few men worked in all London, with pleasure, zeal, hope. . . .

Yes, yes, those were the good days. They did not last long; before and after them were cares, miseries, endurance multiform. I have always felt grateful to Mr. --- of Knightsbridge; he gave me a year of health, and almost of peace.

## XII.

A whole day's walk yesterday with no plan; just a long ramble of hour after hour, entirely enjoyable. It ended at Topsham, where I sat on the little churchyard terrace, and watched the evening tide come up the broad estuary. I have a great liking for Topsham, and that churchyard, overlooking what is not quite sea, yet more than river, is one of the most restful spots I know. Of course the association with old Chaucer, who speaks of Topsham sailors, helps my mood. I came home very tired; but I am not yet decrepit, and for that I must be thankful.

The unspeakable blessedness of having a *home*! Much as my imagination has dwelt upon it for thirty years, I never knew how deep and exquisite a joy could lie in the assurance that one is *at home* for ever. Again and again I come back upon this thought; nothing but Death can oust me from my abiding place. And Death I would fain learn to regard as a friend, who will but intensify the peace I now relish.

When one is at home, how one's affections grow about everything in the neighbourhood! I always thought with fondness of this corner of Devon, but what was that compared with the love which now strengthens in me day by day! Beginning with my house, every stick and stone of it is dear to me as my heart's blood; I find myself laying an affectionate hand on the door-post, giving a pat, as I go by, to the garden gate. Every tree and shrub in the garden is my beloved friend; I touch them, when need is, very tenderly, as though carelessness might pain, or roughness injure them. If I pull up a weed in the walk, I look at it with a certain sadness before throwing it away; it belongs to my home.

And all the country round about. These villages, how delightful are their names to my ear! I find myself reading with interest all the local news in the Exeter paper. Not that I care about the people; with barely one or two exceptions, the people are nothing to me, and the less I see of them the better I am pleased. But the *places* grow ever more dear to me. I like to know of anything that has happened at Heavitree, or Brampford Speke, or Newton St. Cyres. I begin to pride myself on knowing every road and lane, every bridle path and foot-way for miles about. I like to learn the names of farms and of fields. And all this because here is my abiding place, because I am home for ever.

It seems to me that the very clouds that pass above my house are more interesting and beautiful than clouds elsewhere.

And to think that at one time I called myself a socialist, communist, anything you like of the revolutionary kind! Not for long, to be sure, and I suspect that there was always something in me that scoffed when my lips uttered such things. Why, no man living has a more profound sense of property than I; no man ever lived, who was, in every fibre, more vehemently an individualist.

## XIII.

In this high summertide, I remember with a strange feeling that there are people who, of their free choice, spend day and night in cities, who throng to the gabble of drawing-rooms, make festival in public eating-houses, sweat in the glare of the theatre. They call it life; they call it enjoyment. Why, so it is, for them; they are so made. The folly is mine, to wonder that they fulfil their destiny.

But with what deep and quiet thanksgiving do I remind myself that never shall I mingle with that well-millinered and tailored herd! Happily, I never saw much of them. Certain occasions I recall when a supposed necessity took me into their dismal precincts; a sick buzzing in the brain, a languor as of exhausted limbs, comes upon me with the memory. The relief with which I stepped out into the street again, when all was over! Dear to me then was poverty, which for the moment seemed to make me a free man. Dear to me was the labour at my desk, which, by comparison, enabled me to respect myself.

Never again shall I shake hands with man or woman who is not in truth my friend. Never again shall I go to see acquaintances with whom I have no acquaintance. All men my brothers? Nay, thank Heaven, that they are not! I will do harm, if I can help it, to no one; I will wish good to all; but I will make no pretence of personal kindliness where, in the nature of things, it cannot be felt. I have grimaced a smile and pattered unmeaning words to many a person whom I despised or from whom in heart I shrank; I did so because I had not courage to do otherwise. For a man conscious of such weakness, the best is to live apart from the world. Brave Samuel Johnson! One such truth-teller is worth all the moralists and preachers who ever laboured to humanise mankind. Had *he* withdrawn into solitude, it would have been a national loss. Every one of his blunt, fearless words had more value than a whole evangel on the lips of a timidly good man. It is thus that the commonalty, however well clad, should be treated. So seldom does the fool or the ruffian in broadcloth hear his just designation; so seldom is the man found who has a right to address him by it. By the bandying of insults we profit nothing; there can be no useful rebuke which is exposed to a *tu quoque*. But, as the world is, an honest and wise man should have a rough tongue. Let him speak and spare not!

## XIV.

Vituperation of the English climate is foolish. A better climate does not exist—for healthy people; and it is always as regards the average native in sound health that a climate must be judged. Invalids have no right whatever to talk petulantly of the natural changes of the sky; Nature has not *them* in view; let them (if they can) seek exceptional conditions for their exceptional state, leaving behind them many a million of sound, hearty men and women who take the seasons as they come, and profit by each in turn. In its freedom from extremes, in its common clemency, even in its caprice, which at the worst time holds out hope, our island weather compares well with that of other lands. Who enjoys the fine day of spring, summer, autumn, or winter so much as an Englishman? His perpetual talk of the weather is testimony to his keen relish for most of what it offers him; in lands of blue monotony, even as where climatic conditions are plainly evil, such talk does not go on. So, granting that we have bad days not a few, that the east wind takes us by the throat, that the mists get at our joints, that the sun hides his glory too often and too long, it is plain that the result of all comes to good, that it engenders a mood of zest under the most various aspects of heaven, keeps an edge on our appetite for open-air life.

I, of course, am one of the weaklings who, in grumbling at the weather, merely invite compassion. July, this year, is clouded and windy, very cheerless even here in Devon; I fret and shiver and mutter to myself something about southern skies. Pshaw! Were I the average man of my years, I should be striding over Haldon, caring not a jot for the heavy sky, finding a score of compensations for the lack of sun. Can I not have patience? Do I not know that, some morning, the east will open like a bursting bud into warmth and splendour, and the azure depths above will have only the more solace for my starved anatomy because of this protracted disappointment?

## XV.

I have been at the seaside—enjoying it, yes, but in what a doddering, senile sort of way! Is it I who used to drink the strong wind like wine, who ran exultingly along the wet sands and leapt from rock to rock, barefoot, on the slippery seaweed, who breasted the swelling breaker, and shouted with joy as it buried me in gleaming foam? At the seaside I knew no such thing as bad weather; there were but changes of eager mood and full-blooded life. Now, if the breeze blow too roughly, if there come a pelting shower, I must look for shelter, and sit with my cloak about me. It is but a new reminder that I do best to stay at home, travelling only in reminiscence.

At Weymouth I enjoyed a hearty laugh, one of the good things not easy to get after middle age. There was a notice of steamboats which ply along the coast, steamboats recommended to the public as being "*replete with lavatories and a ladies' saloon.*" Think how many people read this without a chuckle!

## XVI.

In the last ten years I have seen a good deal of English inns in many parts of the country, and it astonishes me to find how bad they are. Only once or twice have I chanced upon an inn (or, if you like, hotel) where I enjoyed any sort of comfort. More often than not, even the beds are unsatisfactory—either pretentiously huge and choked with drapery, or hard and thinly accoutred. Furnishing is uniformly hideous, and there is either no attempt at ornament (the safest thing) or a villainous taste thrusts itself upon one at every turn. The meals, in general, are coarse and poor in quality, and served with gross slovenliness.

I have often heard it said that the touring cyclist has caused the revival of wayside inns. It may be so, but the touring cyclist seems to be very easily satisfied. Unless we are greatly deceived by the old writers, an English inn used to be a delightful resort, abounding in comfort, and supplied with the best of food; a place, too, where one was sure of welcome at once hearty and courteous. The inns of to-day, in country towns and villages, are not in that good old sense inns at all; they are merely public-houses. The landlord's chief interest is the sale of liquor. Under his roof you may, if you choose, eat and sleep, but what you are expected to do is to drink. Yet, even for drinking, there is no decent accommodation. You will find what is called a bar-parlour, a stuffy and dirty room, with crazy chairs, where only the sodden dram-gulper could imagine himself at ease. Should you wish to write a letter, only the worst pen and the vilest ink is forthcoming; this, even in the "commercial room" of many an inn which seems to depend upon the custom of travelling tradesmen. Indeed, this whole business of innkeeping is incredibly mismanaged. Most of all does the common ineptitude or brutality enrage one when it has possession of an old and picturesque house, such as reminds you of the best tradition, a house which might be made as comfortable as house can be, a place of rest and mirth.

At a public-house you expect public-house manners, and nothing better will meet you at most of the so-called inns or hotels. It surprises me to think in how few instances I have found even the pretence of civility. As a rule, the landlord and landlady are either contemptuously superior or boorishly familiar; the waiters and chambermaids do their work with an indifference which only softens to a condescending interest at the moment of your departure, when, if the tip be thought insufficient, a sneer or a muttered insult speeds you on your way. One inn I remember, where, having to go in and out two or three times in a morning, I always found the front door blocked by the portly forms of two women, the landlady and the barmaid, who stood there chatting and surveying the street. Coming from within the house, I had to call out a request for passage; it was granted with all deliberation, and with not a syllable of apology. This was the best "hotel" in a Sussex market town.

And the food. Here, beyond doubt, there is grave degeneracy. It is impossible to suppose that the old travellers by coach were contented with entertainment such as one gets nowadays at the table of a country hotel. The cooking is wont to be wretched; the quality of the meat and vegetables worse than mediocre. What! Shall one ask in vain at an English inn for an honest chop or steak? Again and again has my appetite been frustrated with an offer of mere sinew and scrag. At a hotel where the charge for lunch was five shillings, I have been sickened with pulpy potatoes and stringy cabbage. The very joint—ribs or sirloin, leg or shoulder—is commonly a poor, underfed, sapless thing, scorched in an oven; and as for the round of beef, it has as good as disappeared—probably because it asks too much skill in the salting. Then again one's breakfast bacon; what intolerable stuff, smelling of saltpetre, has been set before me when I paid the price of the best smoked Wiltshire! It would be mere indulgence of the spirit of grumbling to talk about poisonous tea and washy coffee; every one knows that these drinks cannot be had at public tables; but what if there be real reason for discontent with one's pint of ale? Often, still, that draught from the local brewery is sound and invigorating, but there are grievous exceptions, and no doubt the tendency is here, as in other things—a falling off, a carelessness, if not a calculating dishonesty. I foresee the day when Englishmen will have forgotten how to brew beer; when one's only safety will lie in the draught imported from Munich.

## XVII.

I was taking a meal once at a London restaurant—not one of the great eating-places to which men most resort, but a small establishment on the same model in a quiet neighbourhood—when there entered, and sat down at the next table, a young man of the working class, whose dress betokened holiday. A glance told me that he felt anything but at ease; his mind misgave him as he looked about the long room and at the table before him; and when a waiter came to offer him the card, he stared blankly in sheepish confusion. Some strange windfall, no doubt, had emboldened him to enter for the first time such a place as this, and now that he was here, he heartily wished himself out in the street again. However, aided by the waiter's suggestions, he gave an order for a beef-steak and vegetables. When the dish was served, the poor fellow simply could not make a start upon it; he was embarrassed by the display of knives and forks, by the arrangement of the dishes, by the sauce bottles and the cruet-stand, above all, no doubt, by the assembly of people not of his class, and the unwonted experience of being waited upon by a man with a long shirt-front. He grew red; he made the clumsiest and most futile efforts to transport the meat to his plate; food was there before him, but, like a very Tantalus, he was forbidden to enjoy it. Observing with all discretion, I at length saw him pull out his pocket handkerchief, spread it on the table, and, with a sudden effort, fork the meat off the dish into this receptacle. The waiter, aware by this time of the customer's difficulty, came up and spoke a word to him. Abashed into anger, the young man roughly asked what he had to pay. It ended in the waiter's bringing a newspaper, wherein he helped to wrap up meat and vegetables. Money was flung down, and the victim of a mistaken ambition hurriedly departed, to satisfy his hunger amid less unfamiliar surroundings.

It was a striking and unpleasant illustration of social differences. Could such a thing happen in any country but England? I doubt it. The sufferer was of decent appearance, and, with ordinary self-command, might have taken his meal in the restaurant like any one else, quite unnoticed. But he belonged to a class which, among all classes in the world, is distinguished by native clownishness and by unpliability to novel circumstance. The English lower ranks had need be marked by certain peculiar virtues to atone for their deficiencies in other respects.

## XVIII.

It is easy to understand that common judgment of foreigners regarding the English people. Go about in England as a stranger, travel by rail, live at hotels, see nothing but the broadly public aspect of things, and the impression left upon you will be one of hard egoism, of gruffness and sullenness; in a word, of everything that contrasts most strongly with the ideal of social and civic life. And yet, as a matter of fact, no nation possesses in so high a degree the social and civic virtues. The unsociable Englishman, quotha? Why, what country in the world can show such multifarious, vigorous and cordial co-operation, in all ranks, but especially, of course, among the intelligent, for ends which concern the common good? Unsociable! Why, go where you will in England you can hardly find a man—nowadays, indeed, scarce an educated woman—who does not belong to some alliance, for study or sport, for municipal or national benefit, and who will not be seen, in leisure time, doing his best as a social being. Take the so-called sleepy market-town; it is bubbling with all manner of associated activities, and these of the quite voluntary kind, forms of zealously united effort such as are never dreamt of in the countries supposed to be eminently "social." Sociability does not consist in a readiness to talk at large with the first comer. It is not dependent upon natural grace and suavity; it is compatible, indeed, with thoroughly awkward and all but brutal manners. The English have never (at all events, for some two centuries past) inclined to the purely ceremonial or mirthful forms of sociability; but as regards every prime interest of the community—health and comfort, well-being of body and of soul—their social instinct is supreme.

Yet it is so difficult to reconcile this indisputable fact with that other fact, no less obvious, that your common Englishman seems to have no geniality. From the one point of view, I admire and laud my fellow countryman; from the other, I heartily dislike him and wish to see as little of him as possible. One is wont to think of the English as a genial folk. Have they lost in this respect? Has the century of science and money-making sensibly affected the national character? I think always of my experience at the English inn, where it is impossible not to feel a brutal indifference to the humane features of life; where food is bolted without attention, liquor swallowed out of mere habit, where even good-natured accost is a thing so rare as to be remarkable.

Two things have to be borne in mind: the extraordinary difference of demeanour which exists between the refined and the vulgar English, and the natural difficulty of an Englishman in revealing his true self save under the most favourable circumstances.

So striking is the difference of manner between class and class that the hasty observer might well imagine a corresponding and radical difference of mind and character. In Russia, I suppose, the social extremities are seen to be pretty far apart, but, with that possible exception, I should think no

European country can show such a gap as yawns to the eye between the English gentleman and the English boor. The boor, of course, is the multitude; the boor impresses himself upon the traveller. When relieved from his presence, one can be just to him; one can remember that his virtues—though elementary, and strictly in need of direction—are the same, to a great extent, as those of the well-bred man. He does not represent—though seeming to do so—a nation apart. To understand this multitude, you must get below its insufferable manners, and learn that very fine civic qualities can consist with a personal bearing almost wholly repellent.

Then, as to the dogged reserve of the educated man, why, I have only to look into myself. I, it is true, am not quite a representative Englishman; my self-consciousness, my meditative habit of mind, rather dim my national and social characteristics; but set me among a few specimens of the multitude, and am I not at once aware of that instinctive antipathy, that shrinking into myself, that something like unto scorn, of which the Englishman is accused by foreigners who casually meet him? Peculiar to me is the effort to overcome this first impulse—an effort which often enough succeeds. If I know myself at all, I am not an ungenial man; and yet I am quite sure that many people who have known me casually would say that my fault is a lack of geniality. To show my true self, I must be in the right mood and the right circumstances—which, after all, is merely as much as saying that I am decidedly English.

## XIX.

On my breakfast table there is a pot of honey. Not the manufactured stuff sold under that name in shops, but honey of the hive, brought to me by a neighbouring cottager whose bees often hum in my garden. It gives, I confess, more pleasure to my eye than to my palate; but I like to taste of it, because it is honey.

There is as much difference, said Johnson, between a lettered and an unlettered man as between the living and the dead; and, in a way, it was no extravagance. Think merely how one's view of common things is affected by literary association. What were honey to me if I knew nothing of Hymettus and Hybla?—if my mind had no stores of poetry, no memories of romance? Suppose me town-pent, the name might bring with it some pleasantness of rustic odour; but of what poor significance even that, if the country were to me mere grass and corn and vegetables, as to the man who has never read nor wished to read. For the Poet is indeed a Maker: above the world of sense, trodden by hidebound humanity, he builds that world of his own whereto is summoned the unfettered spirit. Why does it delight me to see the bat flitting at dusk before my window, or to hear the hoot of the owl when all the ways are dark? I might regard the bat with disgust, and the owl either with vague superstition or not heed it at all. But these have their place in the poet's world, and carry me above this idle present.

I once passed a night in a little market-town where I had arrived tired and went to bed early. I slept forthwith, but was presently awakened by I knew not what; in the darkness there sounded a sort of music, and, as my brain cleared, I was aware of the soft chiming of church bells. Why, what hour could it be? I struck a light and looked at my watch. Midnight. Then a glow came over me. "We have heard the chimes at midnight, Master Shallow!" Never till then had *I* heard them. And the town in which I slept was Evesham, but a few miles from Stratford-on-Avon. What if those midnight bells had been to me but as any other, and I had reviled them for breaking my sleep?—Johnson did not much exaggerate.

## XX.

It is the second Jubilee. Bonfires blaze upon the hills, making one think of the watchman on Agamemnon's citadel. (It were more germane to the matter to think of Queen Elizabeth and the Armada.) Though wishing the uproar happily over, I can see the good in it as well as another man. English monarchy, as we know it, is a triumph of English common sense. Grant that men cannot do without an overlord; how to make that over-lordship consist with the largest practical measure of national and individual liberty? We, at all events, have for a time solved the question. For a time only, of course; but consider the history of Europe, and our jubilation is perhaps justified.

For sixty years has the British Republic held on its way under one President. It is wide of the mark to object that other Republics, which change their President more frequently, support the semblance of over-lordship at considerably less cost to the people. Britons are minded for the present that the Head of their State shall be called King or Queen; the name is pleasant to them; it corresponds to a popular sentiment, vaguely understood, but still operative, which is called loyalty. The majority thinking thus, and the system being found to work more than tolerably well, what purpose could be served by an attempt at *novas res*? The nation is content to pay the price; it is the nation's affair. Moreover, who can feel the least assurance that a change to one of the common forms of Republicanism would be for the general advantage? Do we find that countries which have made the experiment are so very much better off than our own in point of stable, quiet government and of national welfare? The theorist scoffs at forms which have survived their meaning, at privilege which will bear no examination, at compromises which sound ludicrous, at submissions which seem contemptible; but let him put forward his practical scheme for making all men rational, consistent, just. Englishmen, I imagine, are not endowed with these qualities in any extraordinary degree. Their strength, politically speaking, lies in a recognition of expediency, complemented by respect for the established fact. One of the facts particularly clear to them is the suitability to their minds, their tempers, their habits, of a system of polity which has been established by the slow effort of generations within this sea-girt realm. They have nothing to do with ideals: they never trouble themselves to think about the Rights of Man. If you talk to them (long enough) about the rights of the shopman, or the ploughman, or the cat's-meat-man, they will lend ear, and, when the facts of any such case have been examined, they will find a way of dealing with them. This characteristic of theirs they call Common Sense. To them, all things considered, it has been of vast service; one may even say that the rest of the world has profited by it not a little. That Uncommon Sense might now and then have stood them even in better stead is nothing to the point. The Englishman deals with things as they are, and first and foremost accepts his own being.

This Jubilee declares a legitimate triumph of the average man. Look back for threescore years, and who shall affect to doubt that the time has been marked by many improvements in the material life of the English people? Often have they been at loggerheads among themselves, but they have never flown at each other's throats, and from every grave dispute has resulted some substantial gain. They are a cleaner people and a more sober; in every class there is a diminution of brutality; education—stand for what it may—has notably extended; certain forms of tyranny have been abolished; certain forms of suffering, due to heedlessness or ignorance, have been abated. True, these are mere details; whether they indicate a solid advance in civilization cannot yet be determined. But assuredly the average Briton has cause to jubilate; for the progressive features of the epoch are such as he can understand and approve, whereas the doubt which may be cast upon its ethical complexion is for him either non-existent or unintelligible. So let cressets flare into the night from all the hills! It is no purchased exultation, no servile flattery. The People acclaims itself, yet not without genuine gratitude and affection towards the Representative of its glory and its power. The Constitutional Compact has been well preserved. Review the record of kingdoms, and say how often it has come to pass that sovereign and people rejoiced together over bloodless victories.

## XXI.

At an inn in the north I once heard three men talking at their breakfast on the question of diet. They agreed that most people ate too much meat, and one of them went so far as to declare that, for his part, he rather preferred vegetables and fruit. "Why," he said, "will you believe me that I sometimes make a breakfast of apples?" This announcement was received in silence; evidently the two listeners didn't quite know what to think of it. Thereupon the speaker, in rather a blustering tone, cried out, "Yes, I can make a very good breakfast on *two or three pounds of apples*."

Wasn't it amusing? And wasn't it characteristic? This honest Briton had gone too far in frankness. 'Tis all very well to like vegetables and fruits up to a certain point; but to breakfast on apples! His companions' silence proved that they were just a little ashamed of him; his confession savoured of poverty or meanness; to right himself in their opinion, nothing better occurred to the man than to protest that he ate apples, yes, but not merely one or two; he ate them largely, *by the pound!* I laughed at the fellow, but I thoroughly understood him; so would every Englishman; for at the root of our being is a hatred of parsimony. This manifests itself in all sorts of ludicrous or contemptible forms, but no less is it the source of our finest qualities. An Englishman desires, above all, to live largely; on that account he not only dreads, but hates and despises, poverty. His virtues are those of the free-handed and warm-hearted opulent man; his weaknesses come of the sense of inferiority (intensely painful and humiliating) which attaches in his mind to one who cannot spend and give; his vices, for the most part, originate in loss of self-respect due to loss of secure position.

## XXII.

For a nation of this temper, the movement towards democracy is fraught with peculiar dangers. Profoundly aristocratic in his sympathies, the Englishman has always seen in the patrician class not merely a social, but a moral, superiority; the man of blue blood was to him a living representative of those potencies and virtues which made his ideal of the worthy life. Very significant is the cordial alliance from old time between nobles and people; free, proud homage on one side answering to gallant championship on the other; both classes working together in the cause of liberty. However great the sacrifices of the common folk for the maintenance of aristocratic power and splendour, they were gladly made; this was the Englishman's religion, his inborn *pietas*; in the depths of the dullest soul moved a perception of the ethic meaning attached to lordship. Your Lord was the privileged being endowed by descent with generous instincts, and possessed of means to show them forth in act. A poor noble was a contradiction in terms; if such a person existed, he could only be spoken of with wondering sadness, as though he were the victim of some freak of nature. The Lord was Honourable, Right Honourable; his acts, his words virtually constituted the code of honour whereby the nation lived.

In a new world, beyond the ocean, there grew up a new race, a scion of England, which shaped its life without regard to the principle of hereditary lordship; and in course of time this triumphant Republic began to shake the ideals of the Motherland. Its civilization, spite of superficial resemblances, is not English; let him who will think it superior; all one cares to say is that it has already shown in a broad picture the natural tendencies of English blood when emancipated from the old cult. Easy to understand that some there are who see nothing but evil in the influence of that vast commonwealth. If it has done us good, assuredly the fact is not yet demonstrable. In old England, democracy is a thing so alien to our traditions and rooted sentiment that the line of its progress seems hitherto a mere track of ruin. In the very word is something from which we shrink; it seems to signify nothing less than a national apostasy, a denial of the faith in which we won our glory. The democratic Englishman is, by the laws of his own nature, in parlous case; he has lost the ideal by which he guided his rude, prodigal, domineering instincts; in place of the Right Honourable, born to noble things, he has set up the mere Plebs, born, more likely than not, for all manner of baseness. And, amid all his show of loud self-confidence, the man is haunted with misgiving.

The task before us is no light one. Can we, whilst losing the class, retain the idea it embodied? Can we English, ever so subject to the material, liberate ourselves from that old association, yet guard its meaning in the sphere of spiritual life? Can we, with eyes which have ceased to look reverently on worn-out symbols, learn to select from among the grey-coated multitude, and place in reverence even higher him who "holds his patent of nobility straight from Almighty God"? Upon that depends the future of England. In days gone by, our very Snob bore testimony after his fashion to our scorn of meanness; he at all events imagined himself to be imitating those who were incapable of a sordid transaction, of a plebeian compliance. But the Snob, one notes, is in the way of degeneracy; he has new exemplars; he speaks a ruder language. Him, be sure, in one form or another, we shall have always with us, and to observe his habits is to note the tenor of the time. If he have at the back of his dim mind no living ideal which lends his foolishness a generous significance, then indeed—*videant consules.*

## XXIII.

A visit from N-. He stayed with me two days, and I wish he could have stayed a third. (Beyond the third day, I am not sure that any man would be wholly welcome. My strength will bear but a certain amount of conversation, even the pleasantest, and before long I desire solitude, which is rest.)

The mere sight of N-, to say nothing of his talk, did me good. If appearances can ever be trusted, there are few men who get more enjoyment out of life. His hardships were never excessive; they did not affect his health or touch his spirits; probably he is in every way a better man for having—as he says—"gone through the mill." His recollection of the time when he had to work hard for a five-pound note, and was not always sure of getting it, obviously lends gusto to his present state of ease. I persuaded him to talk about his successes, and to give me a glimpse of their meaning in solid cash. Last Midsummer day, his receipts for the twelvemonth were more than two thousand pounds. Nothing wonderful, of course, bearing in mind what some men are making by their pen; but very good for a writer who does not address the baser throng. Two thousand pounds in a year! I gazed at him with wonder and admiration.

I have known very few prosperous men of letters; N--- represents for me the best and brightest side of literary success. Say what one will after a lifetime of disillusion, the author who earns largely by honest and capable work is among the few enviable mortals. Think of N---'s existence. No other man could do what he is doing, and he does it with ease. Two, or at most three, hours' work a day—and that by no means every day—suffices to him. Like all who write, he has his unfruitful times, his mental worries, his disappointments, but these bear no proportion to the hours of happy and effective labour. Every time I see him he looks in better health, for of late years he has taken much more exercise, and he is often travelling. He is happy in his wife and children; the thought of all the comforts and pleasures he is able to give them must be a constant joy to him; were he to die, his family is safe from want. He has friends and acquaintances as many as he desires; congenial folk gather at his table; he is welcome in pleasant houses near and far; his praise is upon the lips of all whose praise is worth having. With all this, he has the good sense to avoid manifest dangers; he has not abandoned his privacy, and he seems to be in no danger of being spoilt by good fortune. His work is more to him than a means of earning money; he talks about a book he has in hand almost as freshly and keenly as in the old days, when his annual income was barely a couple of hundred. I note, too, that his leisure is not swamped with the publications of the day; he reads as many old books as new, and keeps many of his early enthusiasms.

He is one of the men I heartily like. That he greatly cares for me I do not suppose, but this has nothing to do with the matter; enough that he likes my society well enough to make a special journey down into Devon. I represent to him, of course, the days gone by, and for their sake he will always feel an interest in me. Being ten years my junior, he must naturally regard me as an old buffer; I notice, indeed, that he is just a little too deferential at moments. He feels a certain respect for some of my work, but thinks, I am sure, that I ceased writing none too soon—which is very true. If I had not been such a lucky fellow—if at this moment I were still toiling for bread—it is probable that he and I would see each other very seldom; for N--- has delicacy, and would shrink from bringing his high-spirited affluence face to face with Grub Street squalor and gloom; whilst I, on the other hand, should hate to think that he kept up my acquaintance from a sense of decency. As it is we are very good friends, quite unembarrassed, and—for a couple of days—really enjoy the sight and hearing of each other. That I am able to give him a comfortable bedroom, and set before him an eatable dinner, flatters my pride. If I chose at any time to accept his hearty invitation, I can do so without moral twinges.

Two thousand pounds! If, at N---'s age, I had achieved that income, what would have been the result upon me? Nothing but good, I know; but what form would the good have taken? Should I have become a social man, a giver of dinners, a member of clubs? Or should I merely have begun, ten years sooner, the life I am living now? That is more likely.

In my twenties I used to say to myself: what a splendid thing it will be *when* I am the possessor of a thousand pounds! Well, I have never possessed that sum—never anything like it—and now never shall. Yet it was not an extravagant ambition, methinks, however primitive.

As we sat in the garden dusk, the scent of our pipes mingling with that of roses, N--- said to me in a laughing tone: "Come now, tell me how you felt when you first heard of your legacy?" And I could not tell him; I had nothing to say; no vivid recollection of the moment would come back to me. I am afraid N--- thought he had been indiscreet, for he passed quickly to another subject. Thinking it over now, I see, of course, that it would be impossible to put into words the feeling of that supreme moment of life. It was not joy that possessed me; I did not exult; I did not lose control of myself in any way. But I remember drawing one or two deep sighs, as if all at once relieved of some distressing burden or constraint. Only some hours after did I begin to feel any kind of agitation. That night I did not close my eyes; the night after I slept longer and more soundly than I remember to have done for a score of years. Once or twice in the first week I had a hysterical feeling; I scarce kept myself from shedding tears. And the strange thing is that it seems to have happened so long ago; I seem to have been a free man for many a twelvemonth, instead of only for two. Indeed, that is what I have often thought about forms of true happiness; the brief are quite as satisfying as those that last long. I wanted, before my death, to enjoy liberty from care, and repose in a place I love. That was granted me; and, had I known it only for one whole year, the sum of my enjoyment would have been no whit less than if I live to savour it for a decade.

## XXIV.

The honest fellow who comes to dig in my garden is puzzled to account for my peculiarities; I often catch a look of wondering speculation in his eye when it turns upon me. It is all because I will not let him lay out flower-beds in the usual way, and make the bit of ground in front of the house really neat and ornamental. At first he put it down to meanness, but he knows by now that that cannot be the explanation. That I really prefer a garden so poor and plain that every cottager would be ashamed of it, he cannot bring himself to believe, and of course I have long since given up trying to explain myself. The good man probably concludes that too many books and the habit of solitude have somewhat affected what he would call my "reasons."

The only garden flowers I care for are the quite old-fashioned roses, sunflowers, hollyhocks, lilies and so on, and these I like to see growing as much as possible as if they were wild. Trim and symmetrical beds are my abhorrence, and most of the flowers which are put into them—hybrids with some grotesque name—Jonesia, Snooksia—hurt my eyes. On the other hand, a garden is a garden, and I would not try to introduce into it the flowers which are my solace in lanes and fields. Foxgloves, for instance—it would pain me to see them thus transplanted.

I think of foxgloves, for it is the moment of their glory. Yesterday I went to the lane which I visit every year at this time, the deep, rutty cart-track, descending between banks covered with giant fronds of the polypodium, and overhung with wych-elm and hazel, to that cool, grassy nook where the noble flowers hang on stems all but of my own height. Nowhere have I seen finer foxgloves. I suppose they rejoice me so because of early memories—to a child it is the most impressive of wild flowers; I would walk miles any day to see a fine cluster, as I would to see the shining of purple loosestrife by the water edge, or white lilies floating upon the still depth.

But the gardener and I understand each other as soon as we go to the back of the house, and get among the vegetables. On that ground he finds me perfectly sane. And indeed I am not sure that the kitchen garden does not give me more pleasure than the domain of flowers. Every morning I step round before breakfast to see how things are "coming on." It is happiness to note the swelling of pods, the healthy vigour of potato plants, aye, even the shooting up of radishes and cress. This year I have a grove of Jerusalem artichokes; they are seven or eight feet high, and I seem to get vigour as I look at the stems which are all but trunks, at the great beautiful leaves. Delightful, too, are the scarlet runners, which have to be propped again and again, or they would break down under the abundance of their yield. It is a treat to me to go among them with a basket, gathering; I feel as though Nature herself showed kindness to me, in giving me such abundant food. How fresh and wholesome are the odours—especially if a shower has fallen not long ago!

I have some magnificent carrots this year—straight, clean, tapering, the colour a joy to look upon.

## XXV.

For two things do my thoughts turn now and then to London. I should like to hear the long note of a master's violin, or the faultless cadence of an exquisite voice, and I should like to see pictures. Music and painting have always meant much to me; here I can enjoy them only in memory.

Of course there is the discomfort of concert-hall and exhibition-rooms. My pleasure in the finest music would be greatly spoilt by having to sit amid a crowd, with some idiot audible on right hand or left, and the show of pictures would give me a headache in the first quarter of an hour. *Non sum qualis eram* when I waited several hours at the gallery door to hear Patti, and knew not a moment's fatigue to the end of the concert; or when, at the Academy, I was astonished to find that it was four o'clock, and I had forgotten food since breakfast. The truth is, I do not much enjoy anything nowadays which I cannot enjoy *alone*. It sounds morose; I imagine the comment of good people if they overheard such a confession. Ought I, in truth, to be ashamed of it?

I always read the newspaper articles on exhibitions of pictures, and with most pleasure when the pictures are landscapes. The mere names of paintings often gladden me for a whole day—those names which bring before the mind a bit of seashore, a riverside, a glimpse of moorland or of woods. However feeble his criticism, the journalist generally writes with appreciation of these subjects; his descriptions carry me away to all sorts of places which I shall never see again with the bodily eye, and I thank him for his unconscious magic. Much better this, after all, than really going to London and seeing the pictures themselves. They would not disappoint me; I love and honour even the least of English landscape painters; but I should try to see too many at once, and fall back into my old mood of tired grumbling at the conditions of modern life. For a year or two I have grumbled little—all the better for me.

## XXVI.

Of late, I have been wishing for music. An odd chance gratified my desire.

I had to go into Exeter yesterday. I got there about sunset, transacted my business, and turned to walk home again through the warm twilight. In Southernhay, as I was passing a house of which the ground-floor windows stood open, there sounded the notes of a piano—chords touched by a skilful hand. I checked my step, hoping, and in a minute or two the musician began to play that nocturne of Chopin which I love best—I don't know how to name it. My heart leapt. There I stood in the thickening dusk, the glorious sounds floating about me; and I trembled with very ecstasy of enjoyment. When silence came, I waited in the hope of another piece, but nothing followed, and so I went my way.

It is well for me that I cannot hear music when I will; assuredly I should not have such intense pleasure as comes to me now and then by haphazard. As I walked on, forgetting all about the distance, and reaching home before I knew I was half way there, I felt gratitude to my unknown benefactor—a state of mind I have often experienced in the days long gone by. It happened at times—not in my barest days, but in those of decent poverty—that some one in the house where I lodged played the piano— and how it rejoiced me when this came to pass! I say "played the piano"— a phrase that covers much. For my own part, I was very tolerant; anything that could by the largest interpretation be called music, I welcomed and was thankful; for even "five-finger exercises" I found, at moments, better than nothing. For it was when I was labouring at my desk that the notes of the instrument were grateful and helpful to me. Some men, I believe, would have been driven frantic under the circumstances; to me, anything like a musical sound always came as a godsend; it tuned my thoughts; it made the words flow. Even the street organs put me in a happy mood; I owe many a page to them—written when I should else have been sunk in bilious gloom.

More than once, too, when I was walking London streets by night, penniless and miserable, music from an open window has stayed my step, even as yesterday. Very well can I remember such a moment in Eaton Square, one night when I was going back to Chelsea, tired, hungry, racked by frustrate passions. I had tramped miles and miles, in the hope of wearying myself so that I could sleep and forget. Then came the piano notes—I saw that there was festival in the house—and for an hour or so I revelled as none of the bidden guests could possibly be doing. And when I reached my poor lodgings, I was no longer envious nor mad with desires, but as I fell asleep I thanked the unknown mortal who had played for me, and given me peace.

## XXVII.

To-day I have read *The Tempest*. It is perhaps the play that I love best, and, because I seem to myself to know it so well, I commonly pass it over in opening the book. Yet, as always in regard to Shakespeare, having read it once more, I find that my knowledge was less complete than I supposed. So it would be, live as long as one might; so it would ever be, whilst one had strength to turn the pages and a mind left to read them.

I like to believe that this was the poet's last work, that he wrote it in his home at Stratford, walking day by day in the fields which had taught his boyhood to love rural England. It is ripe fruit of the supreme imagination, perfect craft of the master hand. For a man whose life's business it has been to study the English tongue, what joy can equal that of marking the happy ease wherewith Shakespeare surpasses, in mere command of words, every achievement of those even who, apart from him, are great? I could fancy that, in *The Tempest*, he wrought with a peculiar consciousness of this power, smiling as the word of inimitable felicity, the phrase of incomparable cadence, was whispered to him by the Ariel that was his genius. He seems to sport with language, to amuse himself with new discovery of its resources. From king to beggar, men of every rank and every order of mind have spoken with his lips; he has uttered the lore of fairyland; now it pleases him to create a being neither man nor fairy, a something between brute and human nature, and to endow its purposes with words. These words, how they smack of the moist and spawning earth, of the life of creatures that cannot rise above the soil! We do not think of it enough; we stint our wonder because we fall short in appreciation. A miracle is worked before us, and we scarce give heed; it has become familiar to our minds as any other of nature's marvels, which we rarely pause to reflect upon.

*The Tempest* contains the noblest meditative passage in all the plays; that which embodies Shakespeare's final view of life, and is the inevitable quotation of all who would sum the teachings of philosophy. It contains his most exquisite lyrics, his tenderest love passages, and one glimpse of fairyland which—I cannot but think—outshines the utmost beauty of *A Midsummer Night's Dream*: Prospero's farewell to the "elves of hills, brooks, standing lakes, and groves." Again a miracle; these are things which cannot be staled by repetition. Come to them often as you will, they are ever fresh as though new minted from the brain of the poet. Being perfect, they can never droop under that satiety which arises from the perception of fault; their virtue can never be so entirely savoured as to leave no pungency of gusto for the next approach.

Among the many reasons which make me glad to have been born in England, one of the first is that I read Shakespeare in my mother tongue. If I try to imagine myself as one who cannot know him face to face, who hears him only speaking from afar, and that in accents which only through the labouring intelligence can touch the living soul, there comes upon me a sense of chill discouragement, of dreary deprivation. I am wont to think that I can read Homer, and, assuredly, if any man enjoys him, it is I; but can I for a moment dream that Homer yields me all his music, that his word is to me as to him who walked by the Hellenic shore when Hellas lived? I know that there reaches me across the vast of time no more than a faint and broken echo; I know that it would be fainter still, but for its blending with those memories of youth which are as a glimmer of the world's primeval glory. Let every land have joy of its poet; for the poet is the land itself, all its greatness and its sweetness, all that incommunicable heritage for which men live and die. As I close the book, love and reverence possess me. Whether does my full heart turn to the great Enchanter, or to the Island upon which he has laid his spell? I know not. I cannot think of them apart. In the love and reverence awakened by that voice of voices, Shakespeare and England are but one.

# AUTUMN

## I.

This has been a year of long sunshine. Month has followed upon month with little unkindness of the sky; I scarcely marked when July passed into August, August into September. I should think it summer still, but that I see the lanes yellow-purfled with flowers of autumn.

I am busy with the hawkweeds; that is to say, I am learning to distinguish and to name as many as I can. For scientific classification I have little mind; it does not happen to fall in with my habits of thought; but I like to be able to give its name (the "trivial" by choice) to every flower I meet in my walks. Why should I be content to say, "Oh, it's a hawkweed"? That is but one degree less ungracious than if I dismissed all the yellow-rayed as "dandelions." I feel as if the flower were pleased by my recognition of its personality. Seeing how much I owe them, one and all, the least I can do is to greet them severally. For the same reason I had rather say "hawkweed" than "hieracium"; the homelier word has more of kindly friendship.

## II.

How the mood for a book sometimes rushes upon one, either one knows not why, or in consequence, perhaps, of some most trifling suggestion. Yesterday I was walking at dusk. I came to an old farmhouse; at the garden gate a vehicle stood waiting, and I saw it was our doctor's gig. Having passed, I turned to look back. There was a faint afterglow in the sky beyond the chimneys; a light twinkled at one of the upper windows. I said to myself, "Tristram Shandy," and hurried home to plunge into a book which I have not opened for I dare say twenty years.

Not long ago, I awoke one morning and suddenly thought of the Correspondence between Goethe and Schiller; and so impatient did I become to open the book that I got up an hour earlier than usual. A book worth rising for; much better worth than old Burton, who pulled Johnson out of bed. A book which helps one to forget the idle or venomous chatter going on everywhere about us, and bids us cherish hope for a world "which has such people in't."

These volumes I had at hand; I could reach them down from my shelves at the moment when I hungered for them. But it often happens that the book which comes into my mind could only be procured with trouble and delay; I breathe regretfully and put aside the thought. Ah! the books that one will never read again. They gave delight, perchance something more; they left a perfume in the memory; but life has passed them by for ever. I have but to muse, and one after another they rise before me. Books gentle and quieting; books noble and inspiring; books that well merit to be pored over, not once but many a time. Yet never again shall I hold them in my hand; the years fly too quickly, and are too few. Perhaps when I lie waiting for the end, some of those lost books will come into my wandering thoughts, and I shall remember them as friends to whom I owed a kindness—friends passed upon the way. What regret in that last farewell!

### III.

Every one, I suppose, is subject to a trick of mind which often puzzles me. I am reading or thinking, and at a moment, without any association or suggestion that I can discover, there rises before me the vision of a place I know. Impossible to explain why that particular spot should show itself to my mind's eye; the cerebral impulse is so subtle that no search may trace its origin. If I am reading, doubtless a thought, a phrase, possibly a mere word, on the page before me serves to awaken memory. If I am otherwise occupied, it must be an object seen, an odour, a touch; perhaps even a posture of the body suffices to recall something in the past. Sometimes the vision passes, and there an end; sometimes, however, it has successors, the memory working quite independently of my will, and no link appearing between one scene and the next.

Ten minutes ago I was talking with my gardener. Our topic was the nature of the soil, whether or not it would suit a certain kind of vegetable. Of a sudden I found myself gazing at—the Bay of Avlona. Quite certainly my thoughts had not strayed in that direction. The picture that came before me caused me a shock of surprise, and I am still vainly trying to discover how I came to behold it.

A happy chance that I ever saw Avlona. I was on my way from Corfu to Brindisi. The steamer sailed late in the afternoon; there was a little wind, and as the December night became chilly, I soon turned in. With the first daylight I was on deck, expecting to find that we were near the Italian port; to my surprise, I saw a mountainous shore, towards which the ship was making at full speed. On inquiry, I learnt that this was the coast of Albania; our vessel not being very seaworthy, and the wind still blowing a little (though not enough to make any passenger uncomfortable), the captain had turned back when nearly half across the Adriatic, and was seeking a haven in the shelter of the snow-topped hills. Presently we steamed into a great bay, in the narrow mouth of which lay an island. My map showed me where we were, and with no small interest I discovered that the long line of heights guarding the bay on its southern side formed the Acroceraunian

Promontory. A little town visible high up on the inner shore was the ancient Aulon.

Here we anchored, and lay all day long. Provisions running short, a boat had to be sent to land, and the sailors purchased, among other things, some peculiarly detestable bread—according to them, *cotto al sole*. There was not a cloud in the sky; till evening, the wind whistled above our heads, but the sea about us was blue and smooth. I sat in hot sunshine, feasting my eyes on the beautiful cliffs and valleys of the thickly-wooded shore. Then came a noble sunset; then night crept gently into the hollows of the hills, which now were coloured the deepest, richest green. A little lighthouse began to shine. In the perfect calm that had fallen, I heard breakers murmuring softly upon the beach.

At sunrise we entered the port of Brindisi.

## IV.

The characteristic motive of English poetry is love of nature, especially of nature as seen in the English rural landscape. From the "Cuckoo Song" of our language in its beginnings to the perfect loveliness of Tennyson's best verse, this note is ever sounding. It is persistent even amid the triumph of the drama. Take away from Shakespeare all his bits of natural description, all his casual allusions to the life and aspects of the country, and what a loss were there! The reign of the iambic couplet confined, but could not suppress, this native music; Pope notwithstanding, there came the "Ode to Evening" and that "Elegy" which, unsurpassed for beauty of thought and nobility of utterance in all the treasury of our lyrics, remains perhaps the most essentially English poem ever written.

This attribute of our national mind availed even to give rise to an English school of painting. It came late; that it ever came at all is remarkable enough. A people apparently less apt for that kind of achievement never existed. So profound is the English joy in meadow and stream and hill, that, unsatisfied at last with vocal expression, it took up the brush, the pencil, the etching tool, and created a new form of art. The National Gallery represents only in a very imperfect way the richness and variety of our landscape work. Were it possible to collect, and suitably to display, the very best of such work in every vehicle, I know not which would be the stronger emotion in an English heart, pride or rapture.

One obvious reason for the long neglect of Turner lies in the fact that his genius does not seem to be truly English. Turner's landscape, even when it presents familiar scenes, does not show them in the familiar light. Neither the artist nor the intelligent layman is satisfied. He gives us glorious visions; we admit the glory—but we miss something which we deem essential. I doubt whether Turner tasted rural England; I doubt whether the spirit of English poetry was in him; I doubt whether the essential significance of the common things which we call beautiful was revealed to his soul. Such doubt does not affect his greatness as a poet in colour and in form, but I suspect that it has always been the cause why England could not love him. If any man whom I knew to be a man of brains confessed to me that he preferred Birket Foster, I should smile—but I should understand.

V.

A long time since I wrote in this book. In September I caught a cold, which meant three weeks' illness.

I have not been suffering; merely feverish and weak and unable to use my mind for anything but a daily hour or two of the lightest reading. The weather has not favoured my recovery, wet winds often blowing, and not much sun. Lying in bed, I have watched the sky, studied the clouds, which—so long as they are clouds indeed, and not a mere waste of grey vapour—always have their beauty. Inability to read has always been my horror; once, a trouble of the eyes all but drove me mad with fear of blindness; but I find that in my present circumstances, in my own still house, with no intrusion to be dreaded, with no task or care to worry me, I can fleet the time not unpleasantly even without help of books. Reverie, unknown to me in the days of bondage, has brought me solace; I hope it has a little advanced me in wisdom.

For not, surely, by deliberate effort of thought does a man grow wise. The truths of life are not discovered by us. At moments unforeseen, some gracious influence descends upon the soul, touching it to an emotion which, we know not how, the mind transmutes into thought. This can happen only in a calm of the senses, a surrender of the whole being to passionless contemplation. I understand, now, the intellectual mood of the quietist.

Of course my good housekeeper has tended me perfectly, with the minimum of needless talk. Wonderful woman!

If the evidence of a well-spent life is necessarily seen in "honour, love, obedience, troops of friends," mine, it is clear, has fallen short of a moderate ideal. Friends I have had, and have; but very few. Honour and obedience—why, by a stretch, Mrs. M--- may perchance represent these blessings. As for love—?

Let me tell myself the truth. Do I really believe that at any time of my life I have been the kind of man who merits affection? I think not. I have always been much too self-absorbed; too critical of all about me; too unreasonably proud. Such men as I live and die alone, however much in appearance accompanied. I do not repine at it; nay, lying day after day in solitude and silence, I have felt glad that it was so. At least I give no one trouble, and that is much. Most solemnly do I hope that in the latter days no long illness awaits me. May I pass quickly from this life of quiet enjoyment to the final peace. So shall no one think of me with pained sympathy or with weariness. One—two—even three may possibly feel regret, come the end how it may, but I do not flatter myself that to them I am more than an object of kindly thought at long intervals. It is enough; it signifies that I have not erred wholly. And when I think that my daily life testifies to an act of kindness such as I could never have dreamt of meriting from the man who performed it, may I not be much more than content?

## VI.

How I envy those who become prudent without thwackings of experience! Such men seem to be not uncommon. I don't mean cold-blooded calculators of profit and loss in life's possibilities; nor yet the plodding dull, who never have imagination enough to quit the beaten track of security; but bright-witted and large-hearted fellows who seem always to be led by common sense, who go steadily from stage to stage of life, doing the right, the prudent things, guilty of no vagaries, winning respect by natural progress, seldom needing aid themselves, often helpful to others, and, through all, good-tempered, deliberate, happy. How I envy them!

For of myself it might be said that whatever folly is possible to a moneyless man, that folly I have at one time or another committed. Within my nature there seemed to be no faculty of rational self-guidance. Boy and man, I blundered into every ditch and bog which lay within sight of my way. Never did silly mortal reap such harvest of experience; never had any one so many bruises to show for it. Thwack, thwack! No sooner had I recovered from one sound drubbing than I put myself in the way of another. "Unpractical" I was called by those who spoke mildly; "idiot"—I am sure—by many a ruder tongue. And idiot I see myself, whenever I glance back over the long, devious road. Something, obviously, I lacked from the beginning, some balancing principle granted to most men in one or another degree. I had brains, but they were no help to me in the common circumstances of life. But for the good fortune which plucked me out of my mazes and set me in paradise, I should no doubt have blundered on to the end. The last thwack of experience would have laid me low just when I was becoming really a prudent man.

## VII.

This morning's sunshine faded amid slow-gathering clouds, but something of its light seems still to linger in the air, and to touch the rain which is falling softly. I hear a pattering upon the still leafage of the garden; it is a sound which lulls, and tunes the mind to calm thoughtfulness.

I have a letter to-day from my old friend in Germany, E. B. For many and many a year these letters have made a pleasant incident in my life; more than that, they have often brought me help and comfort. It must be a rare thing for friendly correspondence to go on during the greater part of a lifetime between men of different nationalities who see each other not twice in two decades. We were young men when we first met in London, poor, struggling, full of hopes and ideals; now we look back upon those far memories from the autumn of life. B. writes to-day in a vein of quiet contentment, which does me good. He quotes Goethe: "*Was man in der Jugend begehrt hat man im Alter die Fülle.*"

These words of Goethe's were once a hope to me; later, they made me shake my head incredulously; now I smile to think how true they have proved in my own case. But what, exactly, do they mean? Are they merely an expression of the optimistic spirit? If so, optimism has to content itself with rather doubtful generalities. Can it truly be said that most men find the wishes of their youth satisfied in later life? Ten years ago, I should have utterly denied it, and could have brought what seemed to me abundant evidence in its disproof. And as regards myself, is it not by mere happy accident that I pass my latter years in such enjoyment of all I most desired? Accident—but there is no such thing. I might just as well have called it an accident had I succeeded in earning the money on which now I live.

From the beginning of my manhood, it is true, I longed for bookish leisure; that, assuredly, is seldom even one of the desires in a young man's heart, but perhaps it is one of those which may most reasonably look for gratification later on. What, however, of the multitudes who aim only at wealth, for the power and the pride and the material pleasures which it represents? We know very well that few indeed are successful in that aim; and, missing it, do they not miss everything? For them, are not Goethe's words mere mockery?

Apply them to mankind at large, and perhaps, after all, they are true. The fact of national prosperity and contentment implies, necessarily, the prosperity and contentment of the greater number of the individuals of which the nation consists. In other words, the average man who is past middle life has obtained what he strove for—success in his calling. As a young man, he would not, perhaps, have set forth his aspirations so moderately, but do they not, as a fact, amount to this? In defence of the optimistic view, one may urge how rare it is to meet with an elderly man who harbours a repining spirit. True; but I have always regarded as a fact of infinite pathos the ability men have to subdue themselves to the conditions of life. Contentment so often means resignation, abandonment of the hope seen to be forbidden.

I cannot resolve this doubt.

## VIII.

I have been reading Sainte-Beuve's *Port Royal*, a book I have often thought of reading, but its length, and my slight interest in that period, always held me aloof. Happily, chance and mood came together, and I am richer by a bit of knowledge well worth acquiring. It is the kind of book which, one may reasonably say, tends to edification. One is better for having lived a while with "Messieurs de Port-Royal"; the best of them were, surely, not far from the Kingdom of Heaven.

Theirs is not, indeed, the Christianity of the first age; we are among theologians, and the shadow of dogma has dimmed those divine hues of the early morning, yet ever and anon there comes a cool, sweet air, which seems not to have blown across man's common world, which bears no taint of mortality.

A gallery of impressive and touching portraits. The great-souled M. de Saint-Cyran, with his vision of Christ restored; M. Le Maître, who, at the summit of a brilliant career, turned from the world to meditation and penitence; Pascal, with his genius and his triumphs, his conflicts of soul and fleshly martyrdom; Lancelot, the good Lancelot, ideal schoolmaster, who wrote grammar and edited classical books; the vigorous Arnauld, doctoral rather than saintly, but long-suffering for the faith that was in him; and all the smaller names—Walon de Beaupuis, Nicole, Hamon—spirits of exquisite humility and sweetness—a perfume rises from the page as one reads about them. But best of all I like M. de Tillemont; I could have wished for myself even such a life as his; wrapped in silence and calm, a life of gentle devotion and zealous study. From the age of fourteen, he said, his intellect had occupied itself with but one subject, that of ecclesiastical history. Rising at four o'clock, he read and wrote until half-past nine in the evening, interrupting his work only to say the Offices of the Church, and for a couple of hours' breathing at mid-day. Few were his absences. When he had to make a journey, he set forth on foot, staff in hand, and lightened the way by singing to himself a psalm or canticle. This man of profound erudition had as pure and simple a heart as ever dwelt in mortal. He loved to stop by the road and talk with children, and knew how to hold their attention whilst teaching them a lesson. Seeing boy or girl in charge of a cow, he would ask: "How is it that you, a little child, are able to control that animal, so much bigger and stronger?" And he would show the reason, speaking of the human soul. All this about Tillemont is new to me; well as I knew his name (from the pages of Gibbon), I thought of him merely as the laborious and accurate compiler of historical materials. Admirable as was his work, the spirit in which he performed it is the thing to dwell upon; he studied for study's sake, and with no aim but truth; to him it was a matter of indifference whether his learning ever became known among men, and at any moment he would have given the fruits of his labour to any one capable of making use of them.

Think of the world in which the Jansenists were living; the world of the Fronde, of Richelieu and Mazarin, of his refulgent Majesty Louis XIV. Contrast Port-Royal with Versailles, and—whatever one's judgment of their religious and ecclesiastical aims—one must needs say that these men lived with dignity. The Great Monarch is, in comparison, a poor, sordid creature. One thinks of Molière refused burial—the king's contemptuous indifference for one who could do no more to amuse him being a true measure of the royal greatness. Face to face with even the least of these grave and pious men, how paltry and unclean are all those courtly figures; not *there* was dignity, in the palace chambers and the stately gardens, but in the poor rooms where the solitaries of Port-Royal prayed and studied and taught. Whether or not the ideal for mankind, their life was worthy of man. And what is rarer than a life to which that praise can be given?

## IX.

It is amusing to note the superficial forms of reaction against scientific positivism. The triumph of Darwin was signalized by the invention of that happy word Agnostic, which had great vogue. But agnosticism, as a fashion, was far too reasonable to endure. There came a rumour of Oriental magic, (how the world repeats itself!) and presently every one who had nothing better to do gossipped about "esoteric Buddhism"—the saving adjective sounded well in a drawing-room. It did not hold very long, even with the novelists; for the English taste this esotericism was too exotic. Somebody suggested that the old table-turning and spirit-rapping, which had homely associations, might be re-considered in a scientific light, and the idea was seized upon. Superstition pranked in the professor's spectacles, it set up a laboratory, and printed grave reports. Day by day its sphere widened. Hypnotism brought matter for the marvel-mongers, and there followed a long procession of words in limping Greek—a little difficult till practice had made perfect. Another fortunate terminologist hit upon the word "psychical"—the *p* might be sounded or not, according to the taste and fancy of the pronouncer—and the fashionable children of a scientific age were thoroughly at ease. "There *must* be something, you know; one always felt that there *must* be something." And now, if one may judge from what one reads, psychical "science" is comfortably joining hands with the sorcery of the Middle Ages. It is said to be a lucrative moment for wizards that peep and that mutter. If the law against fortune-telling were as strictly enforced in the polite world as it occasionally is in slums and hamlets, we should have a merry time. But it is difficult to prosecute a Professor of Telepathy—and how he would welcome the advertisement!

Of course I know very well that all that make use of these words are not in one and the same category. There is a study of the human mind, in health and in disease, which calls for as much respect as any other study conscientiously and capably pursued; that it lends occasion to fribbles and knaves is no argument against any honest tendency of thought. Men whom one cannot but esteem are deeply engaged in psychical investigations, and have convinced themselves that they are brought into touch with phenomena inexplicable by the commonly accepted laws of life. Be it so. They may be on the point of making discoveries in the world beyond sense. For my own part, everything of this kind not only does not interest me; I turn from it with the strongest distaste. If every wonder-story examined by the Psychical Society were set before me with irresistible evidence of its truth, my feeling (call it my prejudice) would undergo no change whatever. No whit the less should I yawn over the next batch, and lay the narratives aside with—yes, with a sort of disgust. "An ounce of civet, good apothecary!" Why it should be so with me I cannot say. I am as indifferent to the facts or fancies of spiritualism as I am, for instance, to the latest mechanical application of electricity. Edisons and Marconis may thrill the world with astounding novelties; they astound me, as every one else, but straightway I forget my astonishment, and am in every respect the man I was before. The thing has simply no concern for me, and I care not a *volt* if to-morrow the proclaimed discovery be proved a journalist's mistake or invention.

Am I, then, a hidebound materialist? If I know myself, hardly that. Once, in conversation with G. A., I referred to his position as that of the agnostic. He corrected me. "The agnostic grants that there *may* be something beyond the sphere of man's knowledge; I can make no such admission. For me, what is called the unknowable is simply the non-existent. We see what is, and we see all." Now this gave me a sort of shock; it seemed incredible to me that a man of so much intelligence could hold such a view. So far am I from feeling satisfied with any explanation, scientific or other, of myself and of the world about me, that not a day goes by but I fall a-marvelling before the mystery of the universe. To trumpet the triumphs of human knowledge seems to me worse than childishness; now, as of old, we know but one thing—that we know nothing. What! Can I pluck the flower by the wayside, and, as I gaze at it, feel that, if I knew all the teachings of histology, morphology, and so on, with regard to it, I should have exhausted its meanings? What is all this but words, words,

words? Interesting, yes, as observation; but, the more interesting, so much the more provocative of wonder and of hopeless questioning. One may gaze and think till the brain whirls—till the little blossom in one's hand becomes as overwhelming a miracle as the very sun in heaven. Nothing to be known? The flower simply a flower, and there an end on't? The man simply a product of evolutionary law, his senses and his intellect merely availing him to take account of the natural mechanism of which he forms a part? I find it very hard to believe that this is the conviction of any human mind. Rather I would think that despair at an insoluble problem, and perhaps impatience with those who pretend to solve it, bring about a resolute disregard of everything beyond the physical fact, and so at length a self-deception which seems obtuseness.

## X.

It may well be that what we call the unknowable will be for ever the unknown. In that thought is there not a pathos beyond words? It may be that the human race will live and pass away; all mankind, from him who in the world's dawn first shaped to his fearful mind an image of the Lord of Life, to him who, in the dusking twilight of the last age, shall crouch before a deity of stone or wood; and never one of that long lineage have learnt the wherefore of his being. The prophets, the martyrs, their noble anguish vain and meaningless; the wise whose thought strove to eternity, and was but an idle dream; the pure in heart whose life was a vision of the living God, the suffering and the mourners whose solace was in a world to come, the victims of injustice who cried to the Judge Supreme—all gone down into silence, and the globe that bare them circling dead and cold through soundless space. The most tragic aspect of such a tragedy is that it is not unthinkable. The soul revolts, but dare not see in this revolt the assurance of its higher destiny. Viewing our life thus, is it not easier to believe that the tragedy is played with no spectator? And of a truth, of a truth, what spectator can there be? The day may come when, to all who live, the Name of Names will be but an empty symbol, rejected by reason and by faith. Yet the tragedy will be played on.

It is not, I say, unthinkable; but that is not the same thing as to declare that life has no meaning beyond the sense it bears to human intelligence. The intelligence itself rejects such a supposition; in my case, with impatience and scorn. No theory of the world which ever came to my knowledge is to me for one moment acceptable; the possibility of an explanation which would set my mind at rest is to me inconceivable; no whit the less am I convinced that there is a Reason of the All; one which transcends my understanding, one no glimmer of which will ever touch my apprehension; a Reason which must imply a creative power, and therefore, even whilst a necessity of my thought, is by the same criticized into nothing. A like antinomy with that which affects our conception of the infinite in time and space. Whether the rational processes have reached their final development, who shall say? Perhaps what seem to us the impassable limits of thought are but the conditions of a yet early stage in the history of man. Those who make them a proof of a "future state" must necessarily suppose gradations in that futurity; does the savage, scarce risen above the brute, enter upon the same "new life" as the man of highest civilization? Such gropings of the mind certify our ignorance; the strange thing is that they can be held by any one to demonstrate that our ignorance is final knowledge.

## XI.

Yet that, perhaps, will be the mind of coming man; if not the final attainment of his intellectual progress, at all events a long period of self-satisfaction, assumed as finality. We talk of the "ever aspiring soul"; we take for granted that if one religion passes away, another must arise. But what if man presently find himself without spiritual needs? Such modification of his being cannot be deemed impossible; many signs of our life to-day seem to point towards it. If the habits of thought favoured by physical science do but sink deep enough, and no vast calamity come to check mankind in its advance to material contentment, the age of true positivism may arise. Then it will be the common privilege, "rerum cognoscere causas"; the word supernatural will have no sense; superstition will be a dimly understood trait of the early race; and where now we perceive an appalling Mystery, everything will be lucid and serene as a geometric demonstration. Such an epoch of Reason might be the happiest the world could know. Indeed, it would either be that, or it would never come about at all. For suffering and sorrow are the great Doctors of Metaphysic; and, remembering this, one cannot count very surely upon the rationalist millennium.

## XII.

The free man, says Spinoza, thinks of nothing less often than of death. Free, in his sense of the word, I may not call myself. I think of death very often; the thought, indeed, is ever in the background of my mind; yet free in another sense I assuredly am, for death inspires me with no fear. There was a time when I dreaded it; but that, merely because it meant disaster to others who depended upon my labour; the cessation of being has never in itself had power to afflict me. Pain I cannot well endure, and I do indeed think with apprehension of being subjected to the trial of long deathbed torments. It is a sorry thing that the man who has fronted destiny with something of manly calm throughout a life of stress and of striving, may, when he nears the end, be dishonoured by a weakness which is mere disease. But happily I am not often troubled by that dark anticipation.

I always turn out of my way to walk through a country churchyard; these rural resting-places are as attractive to me as a town cemetery is repugnant. I read the names upon the stones, and find a deep solace in thinking that for all these the fret and the fear of life are over. There comes to me no touch of sadness; whether it be a little child or an aged man, I have the same sense of happy accomplishment; the end having come, and with it the eternal peace, what matter if it came late or soon? There is no such gratulation as *Hic jacet*. There is no such dignity as that of death. In the path trodden by the noblest of mankind these have followed; that which of all who live is the utmost thing demanded, these have achieved. I cannot sorrow for them, but the thought of their vanished life moves me to a brotherly tenderness. The dead, amid this leafy silence, seem to whisper encouragement to him whose fate yet lingers: As we are, so shalt thou be; and behold our quiet!

## XIII.

Many a time, when life went hard with me, I have betaken myself to the Stoics, and not all in vain. Marcus Aurelius has often been one of my bedside books; I have read him in the night watches, when I could not sleep for misery, and when assuredly I could have read nothing else. He did not remove my burden; his proofs of the vanity of earthly troubles availed me nothing; but there was a soothing harmony in his thought which partly lulled my mind, and the mere wish that I could find strength to emulate that high example (though I knew that I never should) was in itself a safeguard against the baser impulses of wretchedness. I read him still, but with no turbid emotion, thinking rather of the man than of the philosophy, and holding his image dear in my heart of hearts.

Of course the intellectual assumption which makes his system untenable by the thinker of our time is: that we possess a knowledge of the absolute. Noble is the belief that by exercise of his reason a man may enter into communion with that Rational Essence which is the soul of the world; but precisely because of our inability to find within ourselves any such sure and certain guidance do we of to-day accept the barren doom of scepticism. Otherwise, the Stoic's sense of man's subordination in the universal scheme, and of the all-ruling destiny, brings him into touch with our own philosophical views, and his doctrine concerning the "sociable" nature of man, of the reciprocal obligations which exist between all who live, are entirely congenial to the better spirit of our day. His fatalism is not mere resignation; one has not only to accept one's lot, whatever it is, as inevitable, but to accept it with joy, with praises. Why are we here? For the same reason that has brought about the existence of a horse, or of a vine, to play the part allotted to us by Nature. As it is within our power to understand the order of things, so are we capable of guiding ourselves in accordance therewith; the will, powerless over circumstance, is free to determine the habits of the soul. The first duty is self-discipline; its correspondent first privilege is an inborn knowledge of the law of life.

But we are fronted by that persistent questioner who will accept no *a priori* assumption, however noble in its character and beneficent in its tendency. How do we know that the reason of the Stoic is at harmony with the world's law? I, perhaps, may see life from a very different point of view; to me reason may dictate, not self-subdual, but self-indulgence; I may find in the free exercise of all my passions an existence far more consonant with what seems to me the dictate of Nature. I am proud; Nature has made me so; let my pride assert itself to justification. I am strong; let me put forth my strength, it is the destiny of the feeble to fall before me. On the other hand, I am weak and I suffer; what avails a mere assertion that fate is just, to bring about my calm and glad acceptance of this down-trodden doom? Nay, for there is that within my soul which bids me revolt, and cry against the iniquity of some power I know not. Granting that I am compelled to acknowledge a scheme of things which constrains me to this or that, whether I will or no, how can I be sure that wisdom or moral duty lies in acquiescence? Thus the unceasing questioner; to whom, indeed, there is no reply. For our philosophy sees no longer a supreme sanction, and no longer hears a harmony of the universe.

"He that is unjust is also impious. For the Nature of the Universe, having made all reasonable creatures one for another, to the end that they should do one another good; more or less, according to the several persons and occasions; but in no wise hurt one another; it is manifest that he that doth transgress against this her will, is guilty of impiety towards the most ancient and venerable of all the Deities." How gladly would I believe this! That injustice is impiety, and indeed the supreme impiety, I will hold with my last breath; but it were the merest affectation of a noble sentiment if I supported my faith by such a reasoning. I see no single piece of strong testimony that justice is the law of the universe; I see suggestions incalculable tending to prove that it is not. Rather must I apprehend that man, in some inconceivable way, may at his best moments represent a Principle darkly at strife with that which prevails throughout the world as known to us. If the just man be in truth a worshipper of the most ancient of Deities, he must needs suppose, either that the object of his worship belongs to a fallen dynasty, or—what from of old has been his refuge—that the sacred fire which burns within him is an "evidence of things not seen." What if I am incapable of either supposition? There remains the dignity of a hopeless cause—"*sed victa Catoni.*" But how can there sound the hymn of praise?

"That is best for everyone, which the common Nature of all doth send unto everyone, and then is it best, when she doth send it." The optimism of Necessity, and perhaps, the highest wisdom man can attain unto. "Remember that unto reasonable creatures only is it granted that they may willingly and freely submit." No one could be more sensible than I of the persuasiveness of this high theme. The words sing to me, and life is illumined with soft glory, like that of the autumn sunset yonder. "Consider how man's life is but for a very moment of time, and so depart meek and contented: even as if a ripe olive falling should praise the ground that bare her, and give thanks to the tree that begat her." So would I fain think, when the moment comes. It is the mood of strenuous endeavour, but also the mood of rest. Better than the calm of achieved indifference (if that, indeed, is possible to man); better than the ecstasy which contemns the travail of earth in contemplation of bliss to come. But, by no effort attainable. An influence of the unknown powers; a peace that falleth upon the soul like dew at evening.

## XIV.

I have had one of my savage headaches. For a day and a night I was in blind torment. Have at it, now, with the stoic remedy. Sickness of the body is no evil. With a little resolution and considering it as a natural issue of certain natural processes, pain may well be borne. One's solace is, to remember that it cannot affect the soul, which partakes of the eternal nature. This body is but as "the clothing, or the cottage, of the mind." Let flesh be racked; I, the very I, will stand apart, lord of myself.

Meanwhile, memory, reason, every faculty of my intellectual part, is being whelmed in muddy oblivion. Is the soul something other than the mind? If so, I have lost all consciousness of its existence. For me, mind and soul are one, and, as I am too feelingly reminded, that element of my being is *here*, where the brain throbs and anguishes. A little more of such suffering, and I were myself no longer; the body representing me would gesticulate and rave, but I should know nothing of its motives, its fantasies. The very I, it is too plain, consists but with a certain balance of my physical elements, which we call health. Even in the light beginnings of my headache, I was already not myself; my thoughts followed no normal course, and I was aware of the abnormality. A few hours later, I was but a walking disease; my mind—if one could use the word—had become a barrel-organ, grinding in endless repetition a bar or two of idle music.

What trust shall I repose in the soul that serves me thus? Just as much, one would say, as in the senses, through which I know all that I can know of the world in which I live, and which, for all I can tell, may deceive me even more grossly in their common use than they do on certain occasions where I have power to test them; just as much, and no more—if I am right in concluding that mind and soul are merely subtle functions of body. If I chance to become deranged in certain parts of my physical mechanism, I shall straightway be deranged in my wits; and behold that Something in me which "partakes of the eternal" prompting me to pranks which savour little of the infinite wisdom. Even in its normal condition (if I can determine what that is) my mind is obviously the slave of trivial accidents; I eat something that disagrees with me, and of a sudden the whole aspect of life is changed; this impulse has lost its force, and another which before I should not for a moment have entertained, is all-powerful over me. In short, I know just as little about myself as I do about the Eternal Essence, and I have a haunting suspicion that I may be a mere automaton, my every thought and act due to some power which uses and deceives me.

Why am I meditating thus, instead of enjoying the life of the natural man, at peace with himself and the world, as I was a day or two ago? Merely, it is evident, because my health has suffered a temporary disorder. It has passed; I have thought enough about the unthinkable; I feel my quiet returning. Is it any merit of mine that I begin to be in health once more? Could I, by any effort of the will, have shunned this pitfall?

## XV.

Blackberries hanging thick upon the hedge bring to my memory something of long ago. I had somehow escaped into the country, and on a long walk began to feel mid-day hunger. The wayside brambles were fruiting; I picked and ate, and ate on, until I had come within sight of an inn where I might have made a meal. But my hunger was satisfied; I had no need of anything more, and, as I thought of it, a strange feeling of surprise, a sort of bewilderment, came upon me. What! Could it be that I had eaten, and eaten sufficiently, *without paying*? It struck me as an extraordinary thing. At that time, my ceaseless preoccupation was how to obtain money to keep myself alive. Many a day I had suffered hunger because I durst not spend the few coins I possessed; the food I could buy was in any case unsatisfactory, unvaried. But here Nature had given me a feast, which seemed delicious, and I had eaten all I wanted. The wonder held me for a long time, and to this day I can recall it, understand it.

I think there could be no better illustration of what it means to be very poor in a great town. And I am glad to have been through it. To those days of misery I owe much of the contentment which I now enjoy; not by mere force of contrast, but because I have been better taught than most men the facts which condition our day to day existence. To the ordinary educated person, freedom from anxiety as to how he shall merely be fed and clothed is a matter of course; questioned, he would admit it to be an agreeable state of things, but it is no more a source of conscious joy to him than physical health to the thoroughly sound man. For me, were I to live another fifty years, this security would be a delightful surprise renewed with every renewal of day. I know, as only one with my experience can, all that is involved in the possession of means to live. The average educated man has never stood alone, utterly alone, just clad and nothing more than that, with the problem before him of wresting his next meal from a world that cares not whether he live or die. There is no such school of political economy. Go through that course of lectures, and you will never again become confused as to the meaning of elementary terms in that sorry science.

I understand, far better than most men, what I owe to the labour of others. This money which I "draw" at the four quarters of the year, in a sense falls to me from heaven; but I know very well that every drachm is sweated from human pores. Not, thank goodness, with the declared tyranny of basest capitalism; I mean only that it is the product of human labour; perhaps wholesome, but none the less compulsory. Look far enough, and it means muscular toil, that swinking of the ruder man which supports all the complex structure of our life. When I think of him thus, the man of the people earns my gratitude. That it is gratitude from afar, that I never was, and never shall be, capable of democratic fervour, is a characteristic of my mind which I long ago accepted as final. I have known revolt against the privilege of wealth (can I not remember spots in London where I have stood, savage with misery, looking at the prosperous folk who passed?), but I could never feel myself at one with the native poor among whom I dwelt. And for the simplest reason; I came to know them too well. He who cultivates his enthusiasm amid graces and comforts may nourish an illusion with regard to the world below him all his life long, and I do not deny that he may be the better for it; for me, no illusion was possible. I knew the poor, and I knew that their aims were not mine. I knew that the kind of life (such a modest life!) which I should have accepted as little short of the ideal, would have been to them—if they could have been made to understand it—a weariness and a contempt. To ally myself with them against the "upper world" would have been mere dishonesty, or sheer despair. What they at heart desired, was to me barren; what I coveted, was to them for ever incomprehensible.

That my own aim indicated an ideal which is the best for all to pursue, I am far from maintaining. It may be so, or not; I have long known the idleness of advocating reform on a basis of personal predilection. Enough to set my own thoughts in order, without seeking to devise a new economy for the world. But it is much to see clearly from one's point of view, and therein the evil days I have treasured are of no little help to me. If my knowledge be only subjective, why, it only concerns myself; I preach to no one. Upon another man, of origin and education like to mine, a like experience of hardship might have a totally different effect; he might identify himself with the poor, burn to the end of his life with the noblest humanitarianism. I should no further criticize him than to say that he saw with other eyes than mine. A vision, perhaps, larger and more just. But in one respect he resembles me. If ever such a man arises, let him be questioned; it will be found that he once made a meal of blackberries—and mused upon it.

## XVI.

I stood to-day watching harvesters at work, and a foolish envy took hold upon me. To be one of those brawny, brown-necked men, who can string their muscles from dawn to sundown, and go home without an ache to the sound slumber which will make them fresh again for to-morrow's toil! I am a man in the middle years, with limbs shaped as those of another, and subject to no prostrating malady, yet I doubt whether I could endure the lightest part of this field labour even for half an hour. Is that indeed to be a man? Could I feel surprised if one of these stalwart fellows turned upon me a look of good-natured contempt? Yet he would never dream that I envied him; he would think it as probable, no doubt, that I should compare myself unfavourably with one of the farm horses.

There comes the old idle dream: balance of mind and body, perfect physical health combined with the fulness of intellectual vigour. Why should I not be there in the harvest field, if so it pleased me, yet none the less live for thought? Many a theorist holds the thing possible, and looks to its coming in a better time. If so, two changes must needs come before it; there will no longer exist a profession of literature, and all but the whole of every library will be destroyed, leaving only the few books which are universally recognized as national treasures. Thus, and thus only, can mental and physical equilibrium ever be brought about.

It is idle to talk to us of "the Greeks." The people we mean when so naming them were a few little communities, living under very peculiar conditions, and endowed by Nature with most exceptional characteristics. The sporadic civilization which we are too much in the habit of regarding as if it had been no less stable than brilliant, was a succession of the briefest splendours, gleaming here and there from the coasts of the Aegean to those of the western Mediterranean. Our heritage of Greek literature and art is priceless; the example of Greek life possesses for us not the slightest value. The Greeks had nothing alien to study—not even a foreign or a dead language. They read hardly at all, preferring to listen. They were a slave-holding people, much given to social amusement, and hardly knowing what we call industry. Their ignorance was vast, their wisdom a grace of the gods. Together with their fair intelligence, they had grave moral weaknesses. If we could see and speak with an average Athenian of the Periclean age, he would cause no little disappointment—there would be so much more of the barbarian in him, and at the same time of the decadent, than we had anticipated. More than possibly, even his physique would be a disillusion. Leave him in that old world, which is precious to the imagination of a few, but to the business and bosoms of the modern multitude irrelevant as Memphis or Babylon.

The man of thought, as we understand him, is all but necessarily the man of impaired health. The rare exception will be found to come of a stock which may, indeed, have been distinguished by intelligence, but represented in all its members the active rather than the studious or contemplative life; whilst the children of such fortunate thinkers are sure either to revert to the active type or to exhibit the familiar sacrifice of body to mind. I am not denying the possibility of *mens sana in corpore sano*; that is another thing. Nor do I speak of the healthy people (happily still numerous) who are at the same time bright-witted and fond of books. The man I have in view is he who pursues the things of the mind with passion, who turns impatiently from all common interests or cares which encroach upon his sacred time, who is haunted by a sense of the infinity of thought and learning, who, sadly aware of the conditions on which he holds his mental vitality, cannot resist the hourly temptation to ignore them. Add to these native characteristics the frequent fact that such a man must make merchandise of his attainments, must toil under the perpetual menace of destitution; and what hope remains that his blood will keep the true rhythm, that his nerves will play as Nature bade them, that his sinews will bide the strain of exceptional task? Such a man may gaze with envy at those who "sweat in the eye of Phoebus," but he knows that no choice was offered him. And if life has so far been benignant as to grant him frequent tranquillity of studious hours, let him look from the reapers to the golden harvest, and fare on in thankfulness.

## XVII.

That a labourer in the fields should stand very much on the level of the beast that toils with him, can be neither desirable nor necessary. He does so, as a matter of fact, and one hears that only the dullest-witted peasant will nowadays consent to the peasant life; his children, taught to read the newspaper, make what haste they can to the land of promise—where newspapers are printed. That here is something altogether wrong it needs no evangelist to tell us; the remedy no prophet has as yet even indicated.

Husbandry has in our time been glorified in eloquence which for the most part is vain, endeavouring, as it does, to prove a falsity—that the agricultural life is, in itself, favourable to gentle emotions, to sweet thoughtfulness, and to all the human virtues. Agriculture is one of the most exhausting forms of toil, and, in itself, by no means conducive to spiritual development; that it played a civilizing part in the history of the world is merely due to the fact that, by creating wealth, it freed a portion of mankind from the labour of the plough. Enthusiasts have tried the experiment of turning husbandman; one of them writes of his experience in notable phrase.

"Oh, labour is the curse of the world, and nobody can meddle with it without becoming proportionately brutified. Is it a praiseworthy matter that I have spent five golden months in providing food for cows and horses? It is not so."

Thus Nathaniel Hawthorne, at Brook Farm. In the bitterness of his disillusion he went too far. Labour may be, and very often is, an accursed and a brutalizing thing, but assuredly, it is not the curse of the world; nay, it is the world's supreme blessing. Hawthorne had committed a folly, and he paid for it in loss of mental balance. For him, plainly, it was no suitable task to feed cows and horses; yet many a man would perceive the nobler side of such occupation, for it signifies, of course, providing food for mankind. The interest of this quotation lies in the fact that, all unconsciously, so intelligent a man as Hawthorne had been reduced to the mental state of our agricultural labourers in revolt against the country life. Not only is his intellect in abeyance, but his emotions have ceased to be a true guide. The worst feature of the rustic mind in our day, is not its ignorance or grossness, but its rebellious discontent. Like all other evils, this is seen to be an inevitable outcome of the condition of things; one understands it only too well. The bucolic wants to "better" himself. He is sick of feeding cows and horses; he imagines that, on the pavement of London, he would walk with a manlier tread.

There is no help in visions of Arcadia; yet it is plain fact that in days gone by the peasantry found life more than endurable, and yet were more intelligent than our clod-hoppers who still hold by the plough. They had their folk-songs, now utterly forgotten. They had romances and fairy lore, which their descendants could no more appreciate than an idyll of Theocritus. Ah, but let it be remembered that they had also a *home*, and this is the illumining word. If your peasant love the fields which give him bread, he will not think it hard to labour in them; his toil will no longer be as that of the beast, but upward-looking and touched with a light from other than the visible heavens. No use to blink the hard and dull features of rustic existence; let them rather be insisted upon, that those who own and derive profit from the land may be constant in human care for the lives which make it fruitful. Such care may perchance avail, in some degree, to counteract the restless tendency of the time; the dweller in a pleasant cottage is not so likely to wish to wander from it as he who shelters himself in a hovel. Well-meaning folk talk about reawakening love of the country by means of deliberate instruction. Lies any hope that way? Does it seem to promise a return of the time when the old English names of all our flowers were common on rustic lips—by which, indeed, they were first uttered? The fact that flowers and birds are well-nigh forgotten, together with the songs and the elves, shows how advanced is the process of rural degeneration. Most likely it is foolishness to hope for the revival of any bygone social virtue. The husbandman of the future will be, I daresay, a well-paid mechanic, of the engine-driver species; as he goes about his work he will sing the last refrain of the music-hall, and his oft-recurring holidays will be spent in the nearest great town. For him, I fancy, there will be little attraction in ever such melodious talk about "common objects of the country." Flowers, perhaps, at all events those of tilth and pasture, will have been all but improved away. And, as likely as not, the word Home will have only a special significance, indicating the common abode of retired labourers who are drawing old-age pensions.

## XVIII.

I cannot close my eyes upon this day without setting down some record of it; yet the foolish insufficiency of words! At sunrise I looked forth; nowhere could I discern a cloud the size of a man's hand; the leaves quivered gently, as if with joy in the divine morning which glistened upon their dew. At sunset I stood in the meadow above my house, and watched the red orb sink into purple mist, whilst in the violet heaven behind me rose the perfect moon. All between, through the soft circling of the dial's shadow, was loveliness and quiet unutterable. Never, I could fancy, did autumn clothe in such magnificence the elms and beeches; never, I should think, did the leafage on my walls blaze in such royal crimson. It was no day for wandering; under a canopy of blue or gold, where the eye could fall on nothing that was not beautiful, enough to be at one with Nature in dreamy rest. From stubble fields sounded the long caw of rooks; a sleepy crowing ever and anon told of the neighbour farm; my doves cooed above their cot. Was it for five minutes, or was it for an hour, that I watched the yellow butterfly wafted as by an insensible tremor of the air amid the garden glintings? In every autumn there comes one such flawless day. None that I have known brought me a mind so touched to the fitting mood of welcome, and so fulfilled the promise of its peace.

# XIX.

I was at ramble in the lanes, when, from somewhere at a distance, there sounded the voice of a countryman—strange to say—singing. The notes were indistinct, but they rose, to my ear, with a moment's musical sadness, and of a sudden my heart was stricken with a memory so keen that I knew not whether it was pain or delight. For the sound seemed to me that of a peasant's song which I once heard whilst sitting among the ruins of Paestum. The English landscape faded before my eyes. I saw great Doric columns of honey-golden travertine; between them, as I looked one way, a deep strip of sea; when I turned, the purple gorges of the Apennine; and all about the temple, where I sat in solitude, a wilderness dead and still but for that long note of wailing melody. I had not thought it possible that here, in my beloved home, where regret and desire are all but unknown to me, I could have been so deeply troubled by a thought of things far off. I returned with head bent, that voice singing in my memory. All the delight I have known in Italian travel burned again within my heart. The old spell has not lost its power. Never, I know, will it again draw me away from England; but the Southern sunlight cannot fade from my imagination, and to dream of its glow upon the ruins of old time wakes in me the voiceless desire which once was anguish.

In his *Italienische Reise*, Goethe tells that at one moment of his life the desire for Italy became to him a scarce endurable suffering; at length he could not bear to hear or to read of things Italian, even the sight of a Latin book so tortured him that he turned away from it; and the day arrived when, in spite of every obstacle, he yielded to the sickness of longing, and in secret stole away southward. When first I read that passage, it represented exactly the state of my own mind; to think of Italy was to feel myself goaded by a longing which, at times, made me literally ill; I, too, had put aside my Latin books, simply because I could not endure the torment of imagination they caused me. And I had so little hope (nay, for years no shadow of reasonable hope) that I should ever be able to appease my desire. I taught myself to read Italian; that was something. I worked (half-heartedly) at a colloquial phrase-book. But my sickness only grew towards despair.

Then came into my hands a sum of money (such a poor little sum) for a book I had written. It was early autumn. I chanced to hear some one speak of Naples—and only death would have held me back.

# XX.

Truly, I grow aged. I have no longer much delight in wine.

But then, no wine ever much rejoiced me save that of Italy. Wine-drinking in England is, after all, only make-believe, a mere playing with an exotic inspiration. Tennyson had his port, whereto clings a good old tradition; sherris sack belongs to a nobler age; these drinks are not for us. Let him who will, toy with dubious Bordeaux or Burgundy; to get good of them, soul's good, you must be on the green side of thirty. Once or twice they have plucked me from despair; I would not speak unkindly of anything in cask or bottle which bears the great name of wine. But for me it is a thing of days gone by. Never again shall I know the mellow hour *cum regnat rosa, cum madent capilli.* Yet how it lives in memory!

"What call you this wine?" I asked of the temple-guardian at Paestum, when he ministered to my thirst. "*Vino di Calabria,*" he answered, and what a glow in the name! There I drank it, seated against the column of Poseidon's temple. There I drank it, my feet resting on acanthus, my eyes wandering from sea to mountain, or peering at little shells niched in the crumbling surface of the sacred stone. The autumn day declined; a breeze of evening whispered about the forsaken shore; on the far summit lay a long, still cloud, and its hue was that of my Calabrian wine.

How many such moments come back to me as my thoughts wander! Dim little *trattorie* in city byways, inns smelling of the sun in forgotten valleys, on the mountain side, or by the tideless shore, where the grape has given me of its blood, and made life a rapture. Who but the veriest fanatic of teetotalism would grudge me those hours so gloriously redeemed? No draught of wine amid the old tombs under the violet sky but made me for the time a better man, larger of brain, more courageous, more gentle. 'Twas a revelry whereon came no repentance. Could I but live for ever in thoughts and feelings such as those born to me in the shadow of the Italian vine! There I listened to the sacred poets; there I walked with the wise of old; there did the gods reveal to me the secret of their eternal calm. I hear the red rillet as it flows into the rustic glass; I see the purple light upon the hills. Fill to me again, thou of the Roman visage and all but Roman speech! Is not yonder the long gleaming of the Appian Way? Chant in the old measure, the song imperishable

> "dum Capitolium
> Scandet cum tacita virgine pontifex—"

aye, and for how many an age when Pontiff and Vestal sleep in the eternal silence. Let the slave of the iron gods chatter what he will; for him flows no Falernian, for him the Muses have no smile, no melody. Ere the sun set, and the darkness fall about us, fill again!

## XXI.

Is there, at this moment, any boy of twenty, fairly educated, but without means, without help, with nothing but the glow in his brain and steadfast courage in his heart, who sits in a London garret, and writes for dear life? There must be, I suppose; yet all that I have read and heard of late years about young writers, shows them in a very different aspect. No garretteers, these novelists and journalists awaiting their promotion. They eat—and entertain their critics—at fashionable restaurants; they are seen in expensive seats at the theatre; they inhabit handsome flats—photographed for an illustrated paper on the first excuse. At the worst, they belong to a reputable club, and have garments which permit them to attend a garden party or an evening "at home" without attracting unpleasant notice. Many biographical sketches have I read, during the last decade, making personal introduction of young Mr. This or young Miss That, whose book was—as the sweet language of the day will have it—"booming"; but never one in which there was a hint of stern struggle, of the pinched stomach and frozen fingers. I surmise that the path of "literature" is being made too easy. Doubtless it is a rare thing nowadays for a lad whose education ranks him with the upper middle class to find himself utterly without resources, should he wish to devote himself to the profession of letters. And there is the root of the matter; writing has come to be recognized as a profession, almost as cut-and-dried as church or law; a lad may go into it with full parental approval, with ready avuncular support. I heard not long ago of an eminent lawyer, who had paid a couple of hundred per annum for his son's instruction in the art of fiction—yea, the art of fiction—by a not very brilliant professor of that art. Really, when one comes to think of it, an astonishing fact, a fact vastly significant. Starvation, it is true, does not necessarily produce fine literature; but one feels uneasy about these carpet-authors. To the two or three who have a measure of conscience and vision, I could wish, as the best thing, some calamity which would leave them friendless in the streets. They would perish, perhaps. But set that possibility against the all but certainty of their present prospect—fatty degeneration of the soul; and is it not acceptable?

I thought of this as I stood yesterday watching a noble sunset, which brought back to my memory the sunsets of a London autumn, thirty years ago; more glorious, it seems to me, than any I have since beheld. It happened that, on one such evening, I was by the river at Chelsea, with nothing to do except to feel that I was hungry, and to reflect that, before morning, I should be hungrier still. I loitered upon Battersea Bridge—the old picturesque wooden bridge, and there the western sky took hold upon me. Half an hour later, I was speeding home. I sat down, and wrote a description of what I had seen, and straightway sent it to an evening newspaper, which, to my astonishment, published the thing next day—"On Battersea Bridge." How proud I was of that little bit of writing! I should not much like to see it again, for I thought it then so good that I am sure it would give me an unpleasant sensation now. Still, I wrote it because I enjoyed doing so, quite as much as because I was hungry; and the couple of guineas it brought me had as pleasant a ring as any money I ever earned.

## XXII.

I wonder whether it be really true, as I have more than once seen suggested, that the publication of Anthony Trollope's autobiography in some degree accounts for the neglect into which he and his works fell so soon after his death. I should like to believe it, for such a fact would be, from one point of view, a credit to "the great big stupid public." Only, of course, from one point of view; the notable merits of Trollope's work are unaffected by one's knowledge of how that work was produced; at his best he is an admirable writer of the pedestrian school, and this disappearance of his name does not mean final oblivion. Like every other novelist of note, he had two classes of admirers—those who read him for the sake of that excellence which here and there he achieved, and the undistinguishing crowd which found in him a level entertainment. But it would be a satisfaction to think that "the great big stupid" was really, somewhere in its secret economy, offended by that revelation of mechanical methods which made the autobiography either a disgusting or an amusing book to those who read it more intelligently. A man with a watch before his eyes, penning exactly so many words every quarter of an hour—one imagines that this picture might haunt disagreeably the thoughts even of Mudie's steadiest subscriber, that it might come between him or her and any Trollopean work that lay upon the counter.

The surprise was so cynically sprung upon a yet innocent public. At that happy time (already it seems so long ago) the literary news set before ordinary readers mostly had reference to literary work, in a reputable sense of the term, and not, as now, to the processes of "literary" manufacture and the ups and downs of the "literary" market. Trollope himself tells how he surprised the editor of a periodical, who wanted a serial from him, by asking how many thousand words it should run to; an anecdote savouring indeed of good old days. Since then, readers have grown accustomed to revelations of "literary" method, and nothing in that kind can shock them. There has come into existence a school of journalism which would seem to have deliberately set itself the task of degrading authorship and everything connected with it; and these pernicious scribblers (or typists, to be more accurate) have found the authors of a fretful age only too receptive of their mercantile suggestions. Yes, yes; I know as well as any man that reforms were needed in the relations between author and publisher. Who knows better than I that your representative author face to face with your representative publisher was, is, and ever will be, at a ludicrous disadvantage? And there is no reason in the nature and the decency of things why this wrong should not by some contrivance be remedied. A big, blusterous, genial brute of a Trollope could very fairly hold his own, and exact at all events an acceptable share in the profits of his work. A shrewd and vigorous man of business such as Dickens, aided by a lawyer who was his devoted friend, could do even better, and, in reaping sometimes more than his publisher, redress the ancient injustice. But pray, what of Charlotte Brontë? Think of that grey, pinched life, the latter years of which would have been so brightened had Charlotte Brontë received but, let us say, one third of what, in the same space of time, the publisher gained by her books. I know all about this; alas! no man better. None the less do I loathe and sicken at the manifold baseness, the vulgarity unutterable, which, as a result of the new order, is blighting our literary life. It is not easy to see how, in such an atmosphere, great and noble books can ever again come into being. May it, perhaps, be hoped that once again the multitude will be somehow touched with disgust?—that the market for "literary" news of this costermonger sort will some day fail?

Dickens. Why, there too was a disclosure of literary methods. Did not Forster make known to all and sundry exactly how Dickens' work was done, and how the bargains for its production were made? The multitudinous public saw him at his desk, learnt how long he sat there, were told that he could not get on without having certain little ornaments before his eyes, and that blue ink and a quill pen were indispensable to his writing; and did all this information ever chill the loyalty of a single reader? There was a difference, in truth, between the picture of Charles Dickens sitting down to a chapter of his current novel, and that of the broad-based Trollope doing his so many words to the fifteen minutes. Trollope, we know, wronged himself by the tone and manner of his reminiscences; but that tone and manner indicated an inferiority of mind, of nature. Dickens—though he died in the endeavour to increase (not for himself) an already ample fortune, disastrous influence of his time and class—wrought with an artistic ingenuousness and fervour such as Trollope could not even conceive. Methodical, of course, he was; no long work of prose fiction was ever brought into existence save by methodical labour; but we know that there was no measuring of so many words to the hour. The picture of him at work which is seen in his own letters is one of the most bracing and inspiring in the history of literature. It has had, and will always have, a great part in maintaining Dickens' place in the love and reverence of those who understand.

## XXIII.

As I walked to-day in the golden sunlight—this warm, still day on the far verge of autumn—there suddenly came to me a thought which checked my step, and for the moment half bewildered me. I said to myself: My life is over. Surely I ought to have been aware of that simple fact; certainly it has made part of my meditation, has often coloured my mood; but the thing had never definitely shaped itself, ready in words for the tongue. My life is over. I uttered the sentence once or twice, that my ear might test its truth. Truth undeniable, however strange; undeniable as the figure of my age last birthday.

My age? At this time of life, many a man is bracing himself for new efforts, is calculating on a decade or two of pursuit and attainment. I, too, may perhaps live for some years; but for me there is no more activity, no ambition. I have had my chance—and I see what I made of it.

The thought was for an instant all but dreadful. What! I, who only yesterday was a young man, planning, hoping, looking forward to life as to a practically endless career, I, who was so vigorous and scornful, have come to this day of definite retrospect? How is it possible? But, I have done nothing; I have had no time; I have only been preparing myself—a mere apprentice to life. My brain is at some prank; I am suffering a momentary delusion; I shall shake myself, and return to common sense—to my schemes and activities and eager enjoyments.

Nevertheless, my life is over.

What a little thing! I knew how the philosophers had spoken; I repeated their musical phrases about the mortal span—yet never till now believed them. And this is all? A man's life can be so brief and so vain? Idly would I persuade myself that life, in the true sense, is only now beginning; that the time of sweat and fear was not life at all, and that it now only depends upon my will to lead a worthy existence. That may be a sort of consolation, but it does not obscure the truth that I shall never again see possibilities and promises opening before me. I have "retired," and for me as truly as for the retired tradesman, life is over. I can look back upon its completed course, and what a little thing! I am tempted to laugh; I hold myself within the limit of a smile.

And that is best, to smile, not in scorn, but in all forbearance, without too much self-compassion. After all, that dreadful aspect of the thing never really took hold of me; I could put it by without much effort. Life is done—and what matter? Whether it has been, in sum, painful or enjoyable, even now I cannot say—a fact which in itself should prevent me from taking the loss too seriously. What does it matter? Destiny with the hidden face decreed that I should come into being, play my little part, and pass again into silence; is it mine either to approve or to rebel? Let me be grateful that I have suffered no intolerable wrong, no terrible woe of flesh or spirit, such as others—alas! alas!—have found in their lot. Is it not much to have accomplished so large a part of the mortal journey with so much ease? If I find myself astonished at its brevity and small significance, why, that is my own fault; the voices of those gone before had sufficiently warned me. Better to see the truth now, and accept it, than to fall into dread surprise on some day of weakness, and foolishly to cry against fate. I will be glad rather than sorry, and think of the thing no more.

## XXIV.

Waking at early dawn used to be one of the things I most dreaded. The night which made me capable of resuming labour had brought no such calm as should follow upon repose; I woke to a vision of the darkest miseries and lay through the hours of daybreak—too often—in very anguish. But that is past. Sometimes, ere yet I know myself, the mind struggles as with an evil spirit on the confines of sleep; then the light at my window, the pictures on my walls, restore me to happy consciousness, happier for the miserable dream. Now, when I lie thinking, my worst trouble is wonder at the common life of man. I see it as a thing so incredible that it oppresses the mind like a haunting illusion. Is it the truth that men are fretting, raving, killing each other, for matters so trivial that I, even I, so far from saint or philosopher, must needs fall into amazement when I consider them? I could imagine a man who, by living alone and at peace, came to regard the everyday world as not really existent, but a creation of his own fancy in unsound moments. What lunatic ever dreamt of things less consonant with the calm reason than those which are thought and done every minute in every community of men called sane? But I put aside this reflection as soon as may be; it perturbs me fruitlessly. Then I listen to the sounds about my cottage, always soft, soothing, such as lead the mind to gentle thoughts. Sometimes I can hear nothing; not the rustle of a leaf, not the buzz of a fly, and then I think that utter silence is best of all.

This morning I was awakened by a continuous sound which presently shaped itself to my ear as a multitudinous shrilling of bird voices. I knew what it meant. For the last few days I have seen the swallows gathering, now they were ranged upon my roof, perhaps in the last council before their setting forth upon the great journey. I know better than to talk about animal instinct, and to wonder in a pitying way at its resemblance to reason. I know that these birds show to us a life far more reasonable, and infinitely more beautiful, than that of the masses of mankind. They talk with each other, and in their talk is neither malice nor folly. Could one but interpret the converse in which they make their plans for the long and perilous flight—and then compare it with that of numberless respectable persons who even now are projecting their winter in the South!

## XXV.

Yesterday I passed by an elm avenue, leading to a beautiful old house. The road between the trees was covered in all its length and breadth with fallen leaves—a carpet of pale gold. Further on, I came to a plantation, mostly of larches; it shone in the richest aureate hue, with here and there a splash of blood-red, which was a young beech in its moment of autumnal glory.

I looked at an alder, laden with brown catkins, its blunt foliage stained with innumerable shades of lovely colour. Near it was a horse-chestnut, with but a few leaves hanging on its branches, and those a deep orange. The limes, I see, are already bare.

To-night the wind is loud, and rain dashes against my casement; to-morrow I shall awake to a sky of winter.

# WINTER

## I.

Blasts from the Channel, with raining scud, and spume of mist breaking upon the hills, have kept me indoors all day. Yet not for a moment have I been dull or idle, and now, by the latter end of a sea-coal fire, I feel such enjoyment of my ease and tranquillity that I must needs word it before going up to bed.

Of course one ought to be able to breast weather such as this of to-day, and to find one's pleasure in the strife with it. For the man sound in body and serene of mind there is no such thing as bad weather; every sky has its beauty, and storms which whip the blood do but make it pulse more vigorously. I remember the time when I would have set out with gusto for a tramp along the wind-swept and rain-beaten roads; nowadays, I should perhaps pay for the experiment with my life. All the more do I prize the shelter of these good walls, the honest workmanship which makes my doors and windows proof against the assailing blast. In all England, the land of comfort, there is no room more comfortable than this in which I sit. Comfortable in the good old sense of the word, giving solace to the mind no less than ease to the body. And never does it look more homely, more a refuge and a sanctuary, than on winter nights.

In my first winter here, I tried fires of wood, having had my hearth arranged for the purpose; but that was a mistake. One cannot burn logs successfully in a small room; either the fire, being kept moderate, needs constant attention, or its triumphant blaze makes the room too hot. A fire is a delightful thing, a companion and an inspiration. If my room were kept warm by some wretched modern contrivance of water-pipes or heated air, would it be the same to me as that beautiful core of glowing fuel, which, if I sit and gaze into it, becomes a world of wonders? Let science warm the heaven-forsaken inhabitants of flats and hotels as effectually and economically as it may; if the choice were forced upon me, I had rather sit, like an Italian, wrapped in my mantle, softly stirring with a key the silver-grey surface of the brasier's charcoal. They tell me we are burning all our coal, and with wicked wastefulness. I am sorry for it, but I cannot on that account make cheerless perhaps the last winter of my life. There may be waste on domestic hearths, but the wickedness is elsewhere—too blatant to call for indication. Use common sense, by all means, in the construction of grates; that more than half the heat of the kindly coal should be blown up the chimney is desired by no one; but hold by the open fire as you hold by whatever else is best in England. Because, in the course of nature, it will be some day a thing of the past (like most other things that are worth living for), is that a reason why it should not be enjoyed as long as possible? Human beings may ere long take their nourishment in the form of pills; the prevision of that happy economy causes me no reproach when I sit down to a joint of meat.

See how friendly together are the fire and the shaded lamp; both have their part alike in the illumining and warming of the room. As the fire purrs and softly crackles, so does my lamp at intervals utter a little gurgling sound when the oil flows to the wick, and custom has made this a pleasure to me. Another sound, blending with both, is the gentle ticking of the clock. I could not endure one of those bustling little clocks which tick like a fever pulse, and are only fit for a stockbroker's office; mine hums very slowly, as though it savoured the minutes no less than I do; and when it strikes, the little voice is silver-sweet, telling me without sadness that another hour of life is reckoned, another of the priceless hours—

"Quae nobis pereunt et imputantur."

After extinguishing the lamp, and when I have reached the door, I always turn to look back; my room is so cosily alluring in the light of the last gleeds, that I do not easily move away. The warm glow is reflected on shining wood, on my chair, my writing-table, on the bookcases, and from the gilt title of some stately volume; it illumes this picture, it half disperses the gloom on that. I could imagine that, as in a fairy tale, the books do but await my departure to begin talking among themselves. A little tongue of flame shoots up from a dying ember; shadows shift upon the ceiling and the walls. With a sigh of utter contentment, I go forth, and shut the door softly.

## II.

I came home this afternoon just at twilight, and, feeling tired after my walk, a little cold too, I first crouched before the fire, then let myself drop lazily upon the hearthrug. I had a book in my hand, and began to read it by the firelight. Rising in a few minutes, I found the open page still legible by the pale glimmer of day. This sudden change of illumination had an odd effect upon me; it was so unexpected, for I had forgotten that dark had not yet fallen. And I saw in the queer little experience an intellectual symbol. The book was verse. Might not the warm rays from the fire exhibit the page as it appears to an imaginative and kindred mind, whilst that cold, dull light from the window showed it as it is beheld by eyes to which poetry has but a poor, literal meaning, or none at all?

## III.

It is a pleasant thing enough to be able to spend a little money without fear when the desire for some indulgence is strong upon one; but how much pleasanter the ability to give money away! Greatly as I relish the comforts of my wonderful new life, no joy it has brought me equals that of coming in aid to another's necessity. The man for ever pinched in circumstances can live only for himself. It is all very well to talk about doing moral good; in practice, there is little scope or hope for anything of that kind in a state of material hardship. To-day I have sent S--- a cheque for fifty pounds; it will come as a very boon of heaven, and assuredly blesseth him that gives as much as him that takes. A poor fifty pounds, which the wealthy fool throws away upon some idle or base fantasy, and never thinks of it; yet to S--- it will mean life and light. And I, to whom this power of benefaction is such a new thing, sign the cheque with a hand trembling, so glad and proud I am. In the days gone by, I have sometimes given money, but with trembling of another kind; it was as likely as not that I myself, some black foggy morning, might have to go begging for my own dire needs. That is one of the bitter curses of poverty; it leaves no right to be generous. Of my abundance—abundance to me, though starveling pittance in the view of everyday prosperity—I can give with happiest freedom; I feel myself a man, and no crouching slave with his back ever ready for the lash of circumstance. There are those, I know, who thank the gods amiss, and most easily does this happen in the matter of wealth. But oh, how good it is to desire little, and to have a little more than enough!

## IV.

After two or three days of unseasonable and depressing warmth, with lowering but not rainy sky, I woke this morning to find the land covered with a dense mist. There was no daybreak, and, till long after the due hour, no light save a pale, sad glimmer at the window; now, at mid-day, I begin dimly to descry gaunt shapes of trees, whilst a haunting drip, drip on the garden soil tells me that the vapour has begun to condense, and will pass in rain. But for my fire, I should be in indifferent spirits on such a day as this; the flame sings and leaps, and its red beauty is reflected in the window-glass. I cannot give my thoughts to reading; if I sat unoccupied, they would brood with melancholy fixedness on I know not what. Better to betake myself to the old mechanic exercise of the pen, which cheats my sense of time wasted.

I think of fogs in London, fogs of murky yellow or of sheer black, such as have often made all work impossible to me, and held me, a sort of dyspeptic owl, in moping and blinking idleness. On such a day, I remember, I once found myself at an end both of coal and of lamp-oil, with no money to purchase either; all I could do was to go to bed, meaning to lie there till the sky once more became visible. But a second day found the fog dense as ever. I rose in darkness; I stood at the window of my garret, and saw that the street was illumined as at night, lamps and shop-fronts perfectly visible, with folk going about their business. The fog, in fact, had risen, but still hung above the house-tops, impermeable by any heavenly beam. My solitude being no longer endurable, I went out, and walked the town for hours. When I returned, it was with a few coins which permitted me to buy warmth and light. I had sold to a second-hand bookseller a volume which I prized, and was so much the poorer for the money in my pocket.

Years after that, I recall another black morning. As usual at such times, I was suffering from a bad cold. After a sleepless night, I fell into a torpor, which held me unconscious for an hour or two. Hideous cries aroused me; sitting up in the dark, I heard men going along the street, roaring news of a hanging that had just taken place. "Execution of Mrs."—I forget the name of the murderess. "Scene on the scaffold!" It was a little after nine o'clock; the enterprising paper had promptly got out its gibbet edition. A morning of midwinter, roofs and ways covered with soot-grimed snow under the ghastly fog-pall; and, whilst I lay there in my bed, that woman had been led out and hanged—hanged. I thought with horror of the possibility that I might sicken and die in that wilderness of houses, nothing above me but "a foul and pestilent congregation of vapours." Overcome with dread, I rose and bestirred myself. Blinds drawn, lamp lit, and by a blazing fire, I tried to make believe that it was kindly night.

## V.

Walking along the road after nightfall, I thought all at once of London streets, and, by a freak of mind, wished I were there. I saw the shining of shop-fronts, the yellow glistening of a wet pavement, the hurrying people, the cabs, the omnibuses—and I wished I were amid it all.

What did it mean, but that I wished I were young again? Not seldom I have a sudden vision of a London street, perhaps the dreariest and ugliest, which for a moment gives me a feeling of home-sickness. Often it is the High Street of Islington, which I have not seen for a quarter of a century, at least; no thoroughfare in all London less attractive to the imagination, one would say; but I see myself walking there—walking with the quick, light step of youth, and there, of course, is the charm. I see myself, after a long day of work and loneliness, setting forth from my lodging. For the weather I care nothing; rain, wind, fog—what does it matter! The fresh air fills my lungs; my blood circles rapidly; I feel my muscles, and have a pleasure in the hardness of the stone I tread upon. Perhaps I have money in my pocket; I am going to the theatre, and, afterwards, I shall treat myself to supper—sausage and mashed potatoes, with a pint of foaming ale. The gusto with which I look forward to each and every enjoyment! At the pit-door, I shall roll and hustle amid the throng, and find it amusing. Nothing tires me. Late at night, I shall walk all the way back to Islington, most likely singing as I go. Not because I am happy—nay, I am anything but that; but my age is something and twenty; I am strong and well.

Put me in a London street this chill, damp night, and I should be lost in barren discomfort. But in those old days, if I am not mistaken, I rather preferred the seasons of bad weather; I had, in fact, the true instinct of townsfolk, which finds pleasure in the triumph of artificial circumstance over natural conditions, delighting in a glare and tumult of busy life under hostile heavens which, elsewhere, would mean shivering ill-content. The theatre, at such a time, is doubly warm and bright; every shop is a happy harbour of refuge—there, behind the counter, stand persons quite at their ease, ready to chat as they serve you; the supper bars make tempting display under their many gas-jets; the public houses are full of people who all have money to spend. Then clangs out the piano-organ—and what could be cheerier!

I have much ado to believe that I really felt so. But then, if life had not somehow made itself tolerable to me, how should I have lived through those many years? Human creatures have a marvellous power of adapting themselves to necessity. Were I, even now, thrown back into squalid London, with no choice but to abide and work there—should I not abide and work? Notwithstanding thoughts of the chemist's shop, I suppose I should.

## VI.

One of the shining moments of my day is that when, having returned a little weary from an afternoon walk, I exchange boots for slippers, out-of-doors coat for easy, familiar, shabby jacket, and, in my deep, soft-elbowed chair, await the tea-tray. Perhaps it is while drinking tea that I most of all enjoy the sense of leisure. In days gone by, I could but gulp down the refreshment, hurried, often harassed, by the thought of the work I had before me; often I was quite insensible of the aroma, the flavour, of what I drank. Now, how delicious is the soft yet penetrating odour which floats into my study, with the appearance of the teapot! What solace in the first cup, what deliberate sipping of that which follows! What a glow does it bring after a walk in chilly rain! The while, I look around at my books and pictures, tasting the happiness of their tranquil possession. I cast an eye towards my pipe; perhaps I prepare it, with seeming thoughtfulness, for the reception of tobacco. And never, surely, is tobacco more soothing, more suggestive of humane thoughts, than when it comes just after tea—itself a bland inspirer.

In nothing is the English genius for domesticity more notably declared than in the institution of this festival—almost one may call it so—of afternoon tea. Beneath simple roofs, the hour of tea has something in it of sacred; for it marks the end of domestic work and worry, the beginning of restful, sociable evening. The mere chink of cups and saucers tunes the mind to happy repose. I care nothing for your five o'clock tea of modish drawing-rooms, idle and wearisome like all else in which that world has part; I speak of tea where one is at home in quite another than the worldly sense. To admit mere strangers to your tea-table is profanation; on the other hand, English hospitality has here its kindliest aspect; never is friend more welcome than when he drops in for a cup of tea. Where tea is really a meal, with nothing between it and nine o'clock supper, it is—again in the true sense—the *homeliest* meal of the day. Is it believable that the Chinese, in who knows how many centuries, have derived from tea a millionth part of the pleasure or the good which it has brought to England in the past one hundred years?

I like to look at my housekeeper when she carries in the tray. Her mien is festal, yet in her smile there is a certain gravity, as though she performed an office which honoured her. She has dressed for the evening; that is to say, her clean and seemly attire of working hours is exchanged for garments suitable to fireside leisure; her cheeks are warm, for she has been making fragrant toast. Quickly her eye glances about my room, but only to have the pleasure of noting that all is in order; inconceivable that anything serious should need doing at this hour of the day. She brings the little table within the glow of the hearth, so that I can help myself without changing my easy position. If she speaks, it will only be a pleasant word or two; should she have anything important to say, the moment will be *after* tea, not before it; this she knows by instinct. Perchance she may just stoop to sweep back a cinder which has fallen since, in my absence, she looked after the fire; it is done quickly and silently. Then, still smiling, she withdraws, and I know that she is going to enjoy her own tea, her own toast, in the warm, comfortable, sweet-smelling kitchen.

## VII.

One has heard much condemnation of the English kitchen. Our typical cook is spoken of as a gross, unimaginative creature, capable only of roasting or seething. Our table is said to be such as would weary or revolt any but gobbet-bolting carnivores. We are told that our bread is the worst in Europe, an indigestible paste; that our vegetables are diet rather for the hungry animal than for discriminative man; that our warm beverages, called coffee and tea, are so carelessly or ignorantly brewed that they preserve no simple virtue of the drink as it is known in other lands. To be sure, there is no lack of evidence to explain such censure. The class which provides our servants is undeniably coarse and stupid, and its handiwork of every kind too often bears the native stamp. For all that, English victuals are, in quality, the best in the world, and English cookery is the wholesomest and the most appetizing known to any temperate clime.

As in so many other of our good points, we have achieved this thing unconsciously. Your ordinary Englishwoman engaged in cooking probably has no other thought than to make the food masticable; but reflect on the results, when the thing is well done, and there appears a culinary principle. Nothing could be simpler, yet nothing more right and reasonable. The aim of English cooking is so to deal with the raw material of man's nourishment as to bring out, for the healthy palate, all its natural juices and savours. And in this, when the cook has any measure of natural or acquired skill, we most notably succeed. Our beef is veritably beef; at its best, such beef as can be eaten in no other country under the sun; our mutton is mutton in its purest essence—think of a shoulder of Southdown at the moment when the first jet of gravy starts under the carving knife! Each of our vegetables yields its separate and characteristic sweetness. It never occurs to us to disguise the genuine flavour of food; if such a process be necessary, then something is wrong with the food itself. Some wiseacre scoffed at us as the people with only one sauce. The fact is, we have as many sauces as we have kinds of meat; each, in the process of cookery, yields its native sap, and this is the best of all sauces conceivable. Only English folk know what is meant by *gravy*; consequently, the English alone are competent to speak on the question of sauce.

To be sure, this culinary principle presupposes food of the finest quality. If your beef and your mutton have flavours scarcely distinguishable, whilst both this and that might conceivably be veal, you will go to work in quite a different way; your object must then be to disguise, to counterfeit, to add an alien relish—in short, to do anything *except* insist upon the natural quality of the viand. Happily, the English have never been driven to these expedients. Be it flesh, fowl, or fish, each comes to table so distinctly and eminently itself that by no possibility could it be confused with anything else. Give your average cook a bit of cod, and tell her to dress it in her own way. The good creature will carefully boil it, and there an end of the matter; and by no exercise of art could she have so treated the fish as to make more manifest and enjoyable that special savour which heaven has bestowed upon cod. Think of our array of joints; how royal is each in its own way, and how utterly unlike any of the others. Picture a boiled leg of mutton. It is mutton, yes, and mutton of the best; nature has bestowed upon man no sweeter morsel; but the same joint roasted is mutton too, and how divinely different! The point is that these differences are natural; that, in eliciting them, we obey the eternal law of things, and no human caprice. Your artificial relish is here not only needless, but offensive.

In the case of veal, we demand "stuffing." Yes, for veal is a somewhat insipid meat, and by experience we have discovered the best method of throwing into relief such inherent goodness as it has. The stuffing does not disguise, nor seek to disguise; it accentuates. Good veal stuffing—reflect!—is in itself a triumph of culinary instinct; so bland it is, and yet so powerful upon the gastric juices.

Did I call veal insipid? I must add that it is only so in comparison with English beef and mutton. When I think of the "brown" on the edge of a really fine cut of veal—!

## VIII.

As so often when my thought has gone forth in praise of things English, I find myself tormented by an after-thought—the reflection that I have praised a time gone by. Now, in this matter of English meat. A newspaper tells me that English beef is non-existent; that the best meat bearing that name has merely been fed up in England for a short time before killing. Well, well; we can only be thankful that the quality is still so good. Real English mutton still exists, I suppose. It would surprise me if any other country could produce the shoulder I had yesterday.

Who knows? Perhaps even our own cookery has seen its best days. It is a lamentable fact that the multitude of English people nowadays never taste roasted meat; what they call by that name is baked in the oven—a totally different thing, though it may, I admit, be inferior only to the right roast. Oh, the sirloin of old times, the sirloin which I can remember, thirty or forty years ago! That was English, and no mistake, and all the history of civilization could show nothing on the table of mankind to equal it. To clap that joint into a steamy oven would have been a crime unpardonable by gods and man. Have I not with my own eyes seen it turning, turning on the spit? The scent it diffused was in itself a cure for dyspepsia.

It is very long since I tasted a slice of boiled beef; I have a suspicion that the thing is becoming rare. In a household such as mine, the "round" is impracticable; of necessity it must be large, altogether too large for our requirements. But what exquisite memories does my mind preserve! The very colouring of a round, how rich it is, yet how delicate, and how subtly varied! The odour is totally distinct from that of roast beef, and yet it is beef incontestable. Hot, of course with carrots, it is a dish for a king; but cold it is nobler. Oh, the thin broad slice, with just its fringe of consistent fat!

We are sparing of condiments, but such as we use are the best that man has invented. And we know *how* to use them. I have heard an impatient innovator scoff at the English law on the subject of mustard, and demand why, in the nature of things, mustard should not be eaten with mutton. The answer is very simple; this law has been made by the English palate— which is impeccable. I maintain it is impeccable! Your educated Englishman is an infallible guide in all that relates to the table. "The man of superior intellect," said Tennyson—justifying his love of boiled beef and new potatoes—"knows what is good to eat"; and I would extend it to all civilized natives of our country. We are content with nothing but the finest savours, the truest combinations; our wealth, and happy natural circumstances, have allowed us an education of the palate of which our natural aptitude was worthy. Think, by the bye, of those new potatoes, just mentioned. Our cook, when dressing them, puts into the saucepan a sprig of mint. This is genius. No otherwise could the flavour of the vegetable be so perfectly, yet so delicately, emphasized. The mint is there, and we know it; yet our palate knows only the young potato.

## IX.

There is to me an odd pathos in the literature of vegetarianism. I remember the day when I read these periodicals and pamphlets with all the zest of hunger and poverty, vigorously seeking to persuade myself that flesh was an altogether superfluous, and even a repulsive, food. If ever such things fall under my eyes nowadays, I am touched with a half humorous compassion for the people whose necessity, not their will, consents to this chemical view of diet. There comes before me a vision of certain vegetarian restaurants, where, at a minim outlay, I have often enough made believe to satisfy my craving stomach; where I have swallowed "savoury cutlet," "vegetable steak," and I know not what windy insufficiencies tricked up under specious names. One place do I recall where you had a complete dinner for sixpence—I dare not try to remember the items. But well indeed do I see the faces of the guests—poor clerks and shopboys, bloodless girls and women of many sorts—all endeavouring to find a relish in lentil soup and haricot something-or-other. It was a grotesquely heart-breaking sight.

I hate with a bitter hatred the names of lentils and haricots—those pretentious cheats of the appetite, those tabulated humbugs, those certificated aridities calling themselves human food! An ounce of either, we are told, is equivalent to—how many pounds?—of the best rump-steak. There are not many ounces of common sense in the brain of him who proves it, or of him who believes it. In some countries, this stuff is eaten by choice; in England only dire need can compel to its consumption. Lentils and haricots are not merely insipid; frequent use of them causes something like nausea. Preach and tabulate as you will, the English palate—which is the supreme judge—rejects this farinaceous makeshift. Even as it rejects vegetables without the natural concomitant of meat; as it rejects oatmeal-porridge and griddle-cakes for a mid-day meal; as it rejects lemonade and ginger-ale offered as substitutes for honest beer.

What is the intellectual and moral state of that man who really believes that chemical analysis can be an equivalent for natural gusto?—I will get more nourishment out of an inch of right Cambridge sausage; aye, out of a couple of ounces of honest tripe; than can be yielded me by half a hundredweight of the best lentils ever grown.

## X.

Talking of vegetables, can the inhabited globe offer anything to vie with the English potato justly steamed? I do not say that it is always—or often—to be seen on our tables, for the steaming of a potato is one of the great achievements of culinary art; but, when it *is* set before you, how flesh and spirit exult! A modest palate will find more than simple comfort in your boiled potato of every day, as served in the decent household. New or old, it is beyond challenge delectable. Try to think that civilized nations exist to whom this food is unknown—nay, who speak of it, on hearsay, with contempt! Such critics, little as they suspect it, never ate a potato in their lives. What they have swallowed under that name was the vegetable with all its exquisite characteristics vulgarized or destroyed. Picture the "ball of flour" (as old-fashioned housewives call it) lying in the dish, diffusing the softest, subtlest aroma, ready to crumble, all but to melt, as soon as it is touched; recall its gust and its after-gust, blending so consummately with that of the joint, hot or cold. Then think of the same potato cooked in any other way, and what sadness will come upon you!

## XI.

It angers me to pass a grocer's shop, and see in the window a display of foreign butter. This is the kind of thing that makes one gloom over the prospects of England. The deterioration of English butter is one of the worst signs of the moral state of our people. Naturally, this article of food would at once betray a decline in the virtues of its maker; butter must be a subject of the dairyman's honest pride, or there is no hope of its goodness. Begin to save your labour, to aim at dishonest profits, to feel disgust or contempt for your work—and the churn declares every one of these vices. They must be very prevalent, for it is getting to be a rare thing to eat English butter which is even tolerable. What! England dependent for dairy-produce upon France, Denmark, America? Had we but one true statesman—but one genuine leader of the people—the ears of English landowners and farmers would ring and tingle with this proof of their imbecility.

Nobody cares. Who cares for anything but the show and bluster which are threatening our ruin? English food, not long ago the best in the world, is falling off in quality, and even our national genius for cooking shows a decline; to anyone who knows England, these are facts significant enough. Foolish persons have prated about "our insular cuisine," demanding its reform on Continental models, and they have found too many like unto themselves who were ready to listen; the result will be, before long, that our excellence will be forgotten, and paltry methods be universally introduced, together with the indifferent viands to which they are suited. Yet, if any generality at all be true, it is a plain fact that English diet and English virtue—in the largest sense of the word—are inseparably bound together.

Our supremacy in this matter of the table came with little taking of thought; what we should now do is to reflect upon the things which used to be instinctive, perceive the reasons of our excellence, and set to work to re-establish it. Of course the vilest cooking in the kingdom is found in London; is it not with the exorbitant growth of London that many an ill has spread over the land? London is the antithesis of the domestic ideal; a social reformer would not even glance in that direction, but would turn all his zeal upon small towns and country districts, where blight may perhaps be arrested, and whence, some day, a reconstituted national life may act upon the great centre of corruption. I had far rather see England covered with schools of cookery than with schools of the ordinary kind; the issue would be infinitely more hopeful. Little girls should be taught cooking and baking more assiduously than they are taught to read. But with ever in view the great English principle—that food is only cooked aright when it yields the utmost of its native and characteristic savour. Let sauces be utterly forbidden—save the natural sauce made of gravy. In the same way with sweets; keep in view the insurpassable English ideals of baked tarts (or pies, if so you call them), and boiled puddings; as they are the wholesomest, so are they the most delicious of sweet cakes yet invented; it is merely a question of having them well made and cooked. Bread, again; we are getting used to bread of poor quality, and ill-made, but the English loaf at its best—such as you were once sure of getting in every village—is the faultless form of the staff of life. Think of the glorious revolution that could be wrought in our troubled England if it could be ordained that no maid, of whatever rank, might become a wife unless she had proved her ability to make and bake a perfect loaf of bread.

## XII.

The good S--- writes me a kindly letter. He is troubled by the thought of my loneliness. That I should choose to live in such a place as this through the summer, he can understand; but surely I should do better to come to town for the winter? How on earth do I spend the dark days and the long evenings?

I chuckle over the good S---'s sympathy. Dark days are few in happy Devon, and such as befall have never brought me a moment's tedium. The long, wild winter of the north would try my spirits; but here, the season that follows autumn is merely one of rest, Nature's annual slumber. And I share in the restful influence. Often enough I pass an hour in mere drowsing by the fireside; frequently I let my book drop, satisfied to muse. But more often than not the winter day is blest with sunshine—the soft beam which is Nature's smile in dreaming. I go forth, and wander far. It pleases me to note changes of landscape when the leaves have fallen; I see streams and ponds which during summer were hidden; my favourite lanes have an unfamiliar aspect, and I become better acquainted with them. Then, there is a rare beauty in the structure of trees ungarmented; and if perchance snow or frost have silvered their tracery against the sober sky, it becomes a marvel which never tires.

Day by day I look at the coral buds on the lime-tree. Something of regret will mingle with my joy when they begin to break.

In the middle years of my life—those years that were the worst of all—I used to dread the sound of a winter storm which woke me in the night. Wind and rain lashing the house filled me with miserable memories and apprehensions; I lay thinking of the savage struggle of man with man, and often saw before me no better fate than to be trampled down into the mud of life. The wind's wail seemed to me the voice of a world in anguish; rain was the weeping of the feeble and the oppressed. But nowadays I can lie and listen to a night-storm with no intolerable thoughts; at worst, I fall into a compassionate sadness as I remember those I loved and whom I shall see no more. For myself, there is even comfort in the roaring dark; for I feel the strength of the good walls about me, and my safety from squalid peril such as pursued me through all my labouring life. "Blow, blow, thou winter wind!" Thou canst not blow away the modest wealth which makes my security. Nor can any "rain upon the roof" put my soul to question; for life has given me all I ever asked—infinitely more than I ever hoped—and in no corner of my mind does there lurk a coward fear of death.

## XIII.

If some stranger from abroad asked me to point out to him the most noteworthy things in England, I should first of all consider his intellect. Were he a man of everyday level, I might indicate for his wonder and admiration Greater London, the Black Country, South Lancashire, and other features of our civilization which, despite eager rivalry, still maintain our modern pre-eminence in the creation of ugliness. If, on the other hand, he seemed a man of brains, it would be my pleasure to take him to one of those old villages, in the midlands or the west, which lie at some distance from a railway station, and in aspect are still untouched by the baser tendencies of the time. Here, I would tell my traveller, he saw something which England alone can show. The simple beauty of the architecture, its perfect adaptation to the natural surroundings, the neatness of everything though without formality, the general cleanness and good repair, the grace of cottage gardens, that tranquillity and security which make a music in the mind of him who gazes—these are what a man must see and feel if he would appreciate the worth and the power of England. The people which has made for itself such homes as these is distinguished, above all things, by its love of order; it has understood, as no other people, the truth that "order is heaven's first law." With order it is natural to find stability, and the combination of these qualities, as seen in domestic life, results in that peculiarly English product, our name for which—though but a pale shadow of the thing itself—has been borrowed by other countries: comfort.

Then Englishman's need of "comfort" is one of his best characteristics; the possibility that he may change in this respect, and become indifferent to his old ideal of physical and mental ease, is the gravest danger manifest in our day. For "comfort," mind you, does not concern the body alone; the beauty and orderliness of an Englishman's home derive their value, nay, their very existence, from the spirit which directs his whole life. Walk from the village to the noble's mansion. It, too, is perfect of its kind; it has the dignity of age, its walls are beautiful, the gardens, the park about it are such as can be found only in England, lovely beyond compare; and all this represents the same moral characteristics as the English cottage, but with greater activities and responsibilities. If the noble grow tired of his mansion, and, letting it to some crude owner of millions, go to live in hotels and hired villas; if the cottager sicken of his village roof, and transport himself to the sixth floor of a "block" in Shoreditch; one sees but too well that the one and the other have lost the old English sense of comfort, and, in losing it, have suffered degradation alike as men and as citizens. It is not a question of exchanging one form of comfort for another; the instinct which made an Englishman has in these cases perished. Perhaps it is perishing from among us altogether, killed by new social and political conditions; one who looks at villages of the new type, at the working-class quarters of towns, at the rising of "flats" among the dwellings of the wealthy, has little choice but to think so. There may soon come a day when, though the word "comfort" continues to be used in many languages, the thing it signifies will be discoverable nowhere at all.

## XIV.

If the ingenious foreigner found himself in some village of manufacturing Lancashire, he would be otherwise impressed. Here something of the power of England might be revealed to him, but of England's worth, little enough. Hard ugliness would everywhere assail his eyes; the visages and voices of the people would seem to him thoroughly akin to their surroundings. Scarcely could one find, in any civilized nation, a more notable contrast than that between these two English villages and their inhabitants.

Yet Lancashire is English, and there among the mill chimneys, in the hideous little street, folk are living whose domestic thoughts claim undeniable kindred with those of the villagers of the kinder south. But to understand how "comfort," and the virtues it implies, can exist amid such conditions, one must penetrate to the hearthside; the door must be shut, the curtain drawn; here "home" does not extend beyond the threshold. After all, this grimy row of houses, ugliest that man ever conceived, is more representative of England to-day than the lovely village among the trees and meadows. More than a hundred years ago, power passed from the south of England to the north. The vigorous race on the other side of Trent only found its opportunity when the age of machinery began; its civilization, long delayed, differs in obvious respects from that of older England. In Sussex or in Somerset, however dull and clownish the typical inhabitant, he plainly belongs to an ancient order of things, represents an immemorial subordination. The rude man of the north is—by comparison—but just emerged from barbarism, and under any circumstances would show less smooth a front. By great misfortune, he has fallen under the harshest lordship the modern world has known—that of scientific industrialism, and all his vigorous qualities are subdued to a scheme of life based upon the harsh, the ugly, the sordid. His racial heritage, of course, marks him to the eye; even as ploughman or shepherd, he differs notably from him of the same calling in the weald or on the downs. But the frank brutality of the man in all externals has been encouraged, rather than mitigated, by the course his civilization has taken, and hence it is that, unless one knows him well enough to respect him, he seems even yet stamped with the half-savagery of his folk as they were a century and a half ago. His fierce shyness, his arrogant self-regard, are notes of a primitive state. Naturally, he never learnt to house himself as did the Southerner, for climate, as well as social circumstance, was unfavourable to all the graces of life. And now one can only watch the encroachment of his rule upon that old, that true England whose strength and virtue were so differently manifested. This fair broad land of the lovely villages signifies little save to the antiquary, the poet, the painter. Vainly, indeed, should I show its beauty and its peace to the observant foreigner; he would but smile, and, with a glance at the traction-engine just coming along the road, indicate the direction of his thoughts.

## XV.

Nothing in all Homer pleases me more than the bedstead of Odysseus. I have tried to turn the passage describing it into English verse, thus:—

> Here in my garth a goodly olive grew;
> Thick was the noble leafage of its prime,
> And like a carven column rose the trunk.
> This tree about I built my chamber walls,
> Laying great stone on stone, and roofed them well,
> And in the portal set a comely door,
> Stout-hinged and tightly closing. Then with axe
> I lopped the leafy olive's branching head,
> And hewed the bole to four-square shapeliness,
> And smoothed it, craftsmanlike, and grooved and pierced,
> Making the rooted timber, where it grew,
> A corner of my couch. Labouring on,
> I fashioned all the bed-frame; which complete,
> The wood I overlaid with shining gear
> Of gold, of silver, and of ivory.
> And last, between the endlong beams I stretched
> Stout thongs of ox-hide, dipped in purple dye.

*Odyssey*, xxiii. 190-201.

Did anyone ever imitate the admirable precedent? Were I a young man, and an owner of land, assuredly I would do so. Choose some goodly tree, straight-soaring; cut away head and branches; leave just the clean trunk and build your house about it in such manner that the top of the rooted timber rises a couple of feet above your bedroom floor. The trunk need not be manifest in the lower part of the house, but I should prefer to have it so; I am a tree-worshipper; it should be as the visible presence of a household god. And how could one more nobly symbolize the sacredness of Home? There can be no home without the sense of permanence, and without home there is no civilization—as England will discover when the greater part of her population have become flat-inhabiting nomads. In some ideal commonwealth, one can imagine the Odyssean bed a normal institution, every head of a household, cottager or lord (for the commonwealth must have its lords, go to!), lying down to rest, as did his fathers, in the Chamber of the Tree. This, one fancies, were a somewhat more fitting nuptial chamber than the chance bedroom of a hotel. Odysseus building his home is man performing a supreme act of piety; through all the ages that picture must retain its profound significance. Note the tree he chose, the olive, sacred to Athena, emblem of peace. When he and the wise goddess meet together to scheme destruction of the princes, they sit ιερης παρα πυθμεν ελαιης. Their talk is of bloodshed, true; but in punishment of those who have outraged the sanctity of the hearth, and to re-establish, after purification, domestic calm and security. It is one of the dreary aspects of modern life that natural symbolism has all but perished. We have no consecrated tree. The oak once held a place in English hearts, but who now reveres it?—our trust is in gods of iron. Money is made at Christmas out of holly and mistletoe, but who save the vendors would greatly care if no green branch were procurable? One symbol, indeed, has obscured all others—the minted round of metal. And one may safely say that, of all the ages since a coin first became the symbol of power, ours is that in which it yields to the majority of its possessors the poorest return in heart's contentment.

## XVI.

I have been dull to-day, haunted by the thought of how much there is that I would fain know, and how little I can hope to learn. The scope of knowledge has become so vast. I put aside nearly all physical investigation; to me it is naught, or only, at moments, a matter of idle curiosity. This would seem to be a considerable clearing of the field; but it leaves what is practically the infinite. To run over a list of only my favourite subjects, those to which, all my life long, I have more or less applied myself, studies which hold in my mind the place of hobbies, is to open vistas of intellectual despair. In an old note-book I jotted down such a list—"things I hope to know, and to know well." I was then four and twenty. Reading it with the eyes of fifty-four, I must needs laugh. There appear such modest items as "The history of the Christian Church up to the Reformation"—"all Greek poetry"—"The field of Mediaeval Romance"—"German literature from Lessing to Heine"—"Dante!" Not one of these shall I ever "know, and know well"; not any one of them. Yet here I am buying books which lead me into endless paths of new temptation. What have I to do with Egypt? Yet I have been beguiled by Flinders Petrie and by Maspéro. How can I pretend to meddle with the ancient geography of Asia Minor? Yet here have I bought Prof. Ramsay's astonishing book, and have even read with a sort of troubled enjoyment a good many pages of it; troubled, because I have but to reflect a moment, and I see that all this kind of thing is mere futile effort of the intellect when the time for serious intellectual effort is over.

It all means, of course, that, owing to defective opportunity, owing, still more perhaps, to lack of method and persistence, a possibility that was in me has been wasted, lost. My life has been merely tentative, a broken series of false starts and hopeless new beginnings. If I allowed myself to indulge that mood, I could revolt against the ordinance which allows me no second chance. *O mihi praeteritos referat si Jupiter annos*! If I could but start again, with only the experience there gained! I mean, make a new beginning of my intellectual life; nothing else, O heaven! nothing else. Even amid poverty, I could do so much better; keeping before my eyes some definite, some not unattainable, good; sternly dismissing the impracticable, the wasteful.

And, in doing so, become perhaps an owl-eyed pedant, to whom would be for ever dead the possibility of such enjoyment as I know in these final years. Who can say? Perhaps the sole condition of my progress to this state of mind and heart which make my happiness was that very stumbling and erring which I so regret.

## XVII.

Why do I give so much of my time to the reading of history? Is it in any sense profitable to me? What new light can I hope for on the nature of man? What new guidance for the direction of my own life through the few years that may remain to me? But it is with no such purpose that I read these voluminous books; they gratify—or seem to gratify—a mere curiosity; and scarcely have I closed a volume, when the greater part of what I have read in it is forgotten.

Heaven forbid that I should remember all! Many a time I have said to myself that I would close the dreadful record of human life, lay it for ever aside, and try to forget it. Somebody declares that history is a manifestation of the triumph of good over evil. The good prevails now and then, no doubt, but how local and transitory is such triumph. If historic tomes had a voice, it would sound as one long moan of anguish. Think steadfastly of the past, and one sees that only by defect of imaginative power can any man endure to dwell with it. History is a nightmare of horrors; we relish it, because we love pictures, and because all that man has suffered is to man rich in interest. But make real to yourself the vision of every blood-stained page—stand in the presence of the ravening conqueror, the savage tyrant—tread the stones of the dungeon and of the torture-room—feel the fire of the stake—hear the cries of that multitude which no man can number, the victims of calamity, of oppression, of fierce injustice in its myriad forms, in every land, in every age—and what joy have you of your historic reading? One would need to be a devil to understand it thus, and yet to delight in it.

Injustice—there is the loathed crime which curses the memory of the world. The slave doomed by his lord's caprice to perish under tortures—one feels it a dreadful and intolerable thing; but it is merely the crude presentment of what has been done and endured a million times in every stage of civilization. Oh, the last thoughts of those who have agonized unto death amid wrongs to which no man would give ear! That appeal of innocence in anguish to the hard, mute heavens! Were there only one such instance in all the chronicles of time, it should doom the past to abhorred oblivion. Yet injustice, the basest, the most ferocious, is inextricable from warp and woof in the tissue of things gone by. And if anyone soothes himself with the reflection that such outrages can happen no more, that mankind has passed beyond such hideous possibility, he is better acquainted with books than with human nature.

It were wiser to spend my hours with the books which bring no aftertaste of bitterness—with the great poets whom I love, with the thinkers, with the gentle writers of pages that soothe and tranquillize. Many a volume regards me from the shelf as though reproachfully; shall I never again take it in my hands? Yet the words are golden, and I would fain treasure them all in my heart's memory. Perhaps the last fault of which I shall cure myself is that habit of mind which urges me to seek knowledge. Was I not yesterday on the point of ordering a huge work of erudition, which I should certainly never have read through, and which would only have served to waste precious days? It is the Puritan in my blood, I suppose, which forbids me to recognise frankly that all I have now to do is to *enjoy*. This is wisdom. The time for acquisition has gone by. I am not foolish enough to set myself learning a new language; why should I try to store my memory with useless knowledge of the past?

Come, once more before I die I will read *Don Quixote*.

## XVIII.

Somebody has been making a speech, reported at a couple of columns' length in the paper. As I glance down the waste of print, one word catches my eye again and again. It's all about "science"—and therefore doesn't concern me.

I wonder whether there are many men who have the same feeling with regard to "science" as I have? It is something more than a prejudice; often it takes the form of a dread, almost a terror. Even those branches of science which are concerned with things that interest me—which deal with plants and animals and the heaven of stars—even these I cannot contemplate without uneasiness, a spiritual disaffection; new discoveries, new theories, however they engage my intelligence, soon weary me, and in some way depress. When it comes to other kinds of science—the sciences blatant and ubiquitous—the science by which men become millionaires—I am possessed with an angry hostility, a resentful apprehension. This was born in me, no doubt; I cannot trace it to circumstances of my life, or to any particular moment of my mental growth. My boyish delight in Carlyle doubtless nourished the temper, but did not Carlyle so delight me because of what was already in my mind? I remember, as a lad, looking at complicated machinery with a shrinking uneasiness which, of course, I did not understand; I remember the sort of disturbed contemptuousness with which, in my time of "examinations," I dismissed "science papers." It is intelligible enough to me, now, that unformed fear: the ground of my antipathy has grown clear enough. I hate and fear "science" because of my conviction that, for long to come if not for ever, it will be the remorseless enemy of mankind. I see it destroying all simplicity and gentleness of life, all the beauty of the world; I see it restoring barbarism under a mask of civilization; I see it darkening men's minds and hardening their hearts; I see it bringing a time of vast conflicts, which will pale into insignificance "the thousand wars of old," and, as likely as not, will whelm all the laborious advances of mankind in blood-drenched chaos.

Yet to rail against it is as idle as to quarrel with any other force of nature. For myself, I can hold apart, and see as little as possible of the thing I deem accursed. But I think of some who are dear to me, whose life will be lived in the hard and fierce new age. The roaring "Jubilee" of last summer was for me an occasion of sadness; it meant that so much was over and gone—so much of good and noble, the like of which the world will not see again, and that a new time of which only the perils are clearly visible, is rushing upon us. Oh, the generous hopes and aspirations of forty years ago! Science, then, was seen as the deliverer; only a few could prophesy its tyranny, could foresee that it would revive old evils and trample on the promises of its beginning. This is the course of things; we must accept it. But it is some comfort to me that I—poor little mortal—have had no part in bringing the tyrant to his throne.

## XIX.

The Christmas bells drew me forth this morning. With but half-formed purpose, I walked through soft, hazy sunshine towards the city, and came into the Cathedral Close, and, after lingering awhile, heard the first notes of the organ, and so entered. I believe it is more than thirty years since I was in an English church on Christmas Day. The old time and the old faces lived again for me; I saw myself on the far side of the abyss of years—that self which is not myself at all, though I mark points of kindred between the beings of then and now. He who in that other world sat to hear the Christmas gospel, either heeded it not at all—rapt in his own visions—or listened only as one in whose blood was heresy. He loved the notes of the organ, but, even in his childish mind, distinguished clearly between the music and its local motive. More than that, he could separate the melody of word and of thought from their dogmatic significance, enjoying the one whilst wholly rejecting the other. "On earth peace, good-will to men"—already that line was among the treasures of his intellect, but only, no doubt, because of its rhythm, its sonority. Life, to him, was a half-conscious striving for the harmonic in thought and speech—and through what a tumult of unmelodious circumstance was he beginning to fight his way!

To-day, I listen with no heretical promptings. The music, whether of organ or of word, is more to me than ever; the literal meaning causes me no restiveness. I felt only glad that I had yielded to the summons of the Christmas bells. I sat among a congregation of shadows, not in the great cathedral, but in a little parish church far from here. When I came forth, it astonished me to see the softly radiant sky, and to tread on the moist earth; my dream expected a wind-swept canopy of cold grey, and all beneath it the gleam of new-fallen snow. It is a piety to turn awhile and live with the dead, and who can so well indulge it as he whose Christmas is passed in no unhappy solitude? I would not now, if I might, be one of a joyous company; it is better to hear the long-silent voices, and to smile at happy things which I alone can remember. When I was scarce old enough to understand, I heard read by the fireside the Christmas stanzas of "In Memoriam." To-night I have taken down the volume, and the voice of so long ago has read to me once again—read as no other ever did, that voice which taught me to know poetry, the voice which never spoke to me but of good and noble things. Would I have those accents overborne by a living tongue, however welcome its sound at another time? Jealously I guard my Christmas solitude.

## XX.

Is it true that the English are deeply branded with the vice of hypocrisy? The accusation, of course, dates from the time of the Round-heads; before that, nothing in the national character could have suggested it. The England of Chaucer, the England of Shakespeare, assuredly was not hypocrite. The change wrought by Puritanism introduced into the life of the people that new element which ever since, more or less notably, has suggested to the observer a habit of double-dealing in morality and religion. The scorn of the Cavalier is easily understood; it created a traditional Cromwell, who, till Carlyle arose, figured before the world as our arch-dissembler. With the decline of genuine Puritanism came that peculiarly English manifestation of piety and virtue which is represented by Mr. Pecksniff—a being so utterly different from Tartufe, and perhaps impossible to be understood save by Englishmen themselves. But it is in our own time that the familiar reproach has been persistently levelled at us. It often sounds upon the lips of our emancipated youth; it is stereotyped for daily impression in the offices of Continental newspapers. And for the reason one has not far to look. When Napoleon called us a "nation of shop-keepers," we were nothing of the kind; since his day we have become so, in the strictest sense of the word; and consider the spectacle of a flourishing tradesman, anything but scrupulous in his methods of business, who loses no opportunity of bidding all mankind to regard him as a religious and moral exemplar. This is the actual show of things with us; this is the England seen by our bitterest censors. There is an excuse for those who charge us with "hypocrisy."

But the word is ill-chosen, and indicates a misconception. The characteristic of your true hypocrite is the assumption of a virtue which not only he has not, but which he is incapable of possessing, and in which he does not believe. The hypocrite may have, most likely has, (for he is a man of brains,) a conscious rule of life, but it is never that of the person to whom his hypocrisy is directed. Tartufe incarnates him once for all. Tartufe is by conviction an atheist and a sensualist; he despises all who regard life from the contrasted point of view. But among Englishmen such an attitude of mind has always been extremely rare; to presume it in our typical money-maker who has edifying sentiments on his lips is to fall into a grotesque error of judgment. No doubt that error is committed by the ordinary foreign journalist, a man who knows less than little of English civilization. More enlightened critics, if they use the word at all, do so carelessly; when speaking with more precision, they call the English "pharisaic"—and come nearer the truth.

Our vice is self-righteousness. We are essentially an Old Testament people; Christianity has never entered into our soul we see ourselves as the Chosen, and by no effort of spiritual aspiration can attain unto humility. In this there is nothing hypocritic. The blatant upstart who builds a church, lays out his money in that way not merely to win social consideration; in his curious little soul he believes (so far as he can believe anything) that what he has done is pleasing to God and beneficial to mankind. He may have lied and cheated for every sovereign he possesses; he may have polluted his life with uncleanness; he may have perpetrated many kinds of cruelty and baseness—but all these things has he done against his conscience, and, as soon as the opportunity comes, he will make atonement for them in the way suggested by such faith as he has, the way approved by public opinion. His religion, strictly defined, is *an ineradicable belief in his own religiousness.* As an Englishman, he holds as birthright the true Piety, the true Morals. That he has "gone wrong" is, alas, undeniable, but never—even when leering most satirically—did he deny his creed. When, at public dinners and elsewhere, he tuned his voice to the note of edification, this man did not utter the lie of the hypocrite he *meant every word he said.* Uttering high sentiments, he spoke, not as an individual, but as an Englishman, and most thoroughly did he believe that all who heard him owed in their hearts allegiance to the same faith. He is, if you like, a Pharisee—but do not misunderstand; his Pharisaism has nothing personal. That would be quite another kind of man; existing, to be sure, in England, but not as a national type. No; he is a Pharisee in the minor degree with regard to those of his countrymen who differ from him in dogma; he is Pharisee absolute with regard to the foreigner. And there he stands, representing an Empire.

The word hypocrisy is perhaps most of all applied to our behaviour in matters of sexual morality, and here with specially flagrant misuse. Multitudes of Englishmen have thrown aside the national religious dogma, but very few indeed have abandoned the conviction that the rules of morality publicly upheld in England are the best known in the world. Any one interested in doing so can but too easily demonstrate that English social life is no purer than that of most other countries. Scandals of peculiar grossness, at no long intervals, give rich opportunity to the scoffer. The streets of our great towns nightly present an exhibition the like of which cannot be seen elsewhere in the world. Despite all this, your average Englishman takes for granted his country's moral superiority, and loses no chance of proclaiming it at the expense of other peoples. To call him hypocrite, is simply not to know the man. He may, for his own part, be gross-minded and lax of life; that has nothing to do with the matter; *he believes in virtue.* Tell him that English morality is mere lip-service, and he will blaze with as honest anger as man ever felt. He is a monument of self-righteousness, again not personal but national.

## XXI.

I make use of the present tense, but am I speaking truly of present England? Such powerful agencies of change have been at work during the last thirty years; and it is difficult, nay impossible, to ascertain in what degree they have affected the national character, thus far. One notes the obvious: decline of conventional religion, free discussion of the old moral standards; therewith, a growth of materialism which favours every anarchic tendency. Is it to be feared that self-righteousness may be degenerating into the darker vice of true hypocrisy? For the English to lose belief in themselves—not merely in their potential goodness, but in their pre-eminence as examples and agents of good—would mean as hopeless a national corruption as any recorded in history. To doubt their genuine worship, in the past, of a very high (though not, of course, the highest) ethical ideal, is impossible for any one born and bred in England; no less impossible to deny that those who are rightly deemed "best" among us, the men and women of gentle or humble birth who are not infected by the evils of the new spirit, still lead, in a very true sense, "honest, sober, and godly" lives. Such folk, one knows, were never in a majority, but of old they had a power which made them veritable representatives of the English *ethos*. If they thought highly of themselves, why, the fact justified them; if they spoke, at times, as Pharisees, it was a fault of temper which carried with it no grave condemnation. Hypocrisy was, of all forms of baseness, that which they most abhorred. So is it still with their descendants. Whether these continue to speak among us with authority, no man can certainly say. If their power is lost, and those who talk of English hypocrisy no longer use the word amiss, we shall soon know it.

## XXII.

It is time that we gave a second thought to Puritanism. In the heyday of release from forms which had lost their meaning, it was natural to look back on that period of our history with eyes that saw in it nothing but fanatical excess; we approved the picturesque phrase which showed the English mind going into prison and having the key turned upon it. Now, when the peril of emancipation becomes as manifest as was the hardship of restraint, we shall do well to remember all the good that lay in that stern Puritan discipline, how it renewed the spiritual vitality of our race, and made for the civic freedom which is our highest national privilege. An age of intellectual glory is wont to be paid for in the general decline of that which follows. Imagine England under Stuart rule, with no faith but the Protestantism of the Tudor. Imagine (not to think of worse) English literature represented by Cowley, and the name of Milton unknown. The Puritan came as the physician; he brought his tonic at the moment when lassitude and supineness would naturally have followed upon a supreme display of racial vitality. Regret, if you will, that England turned for her religion to the books of Israel; this suddenly revealed sympathy of our race with a fierce Oriental theocracy is perhaps not difficult to explain, but one cannot help wishing that its piety had taken another form; later, there had to come the "exodus from Houndsditch," with how much conflict and misery! Such, however, was the price of the soul's health; we must accept the fact, and be content to see its better meaning. Health, of course, in speaking of mankind, is always a relative term. From the point of view of a conceivable civilization, Puritan England was lamentably ailing; but we must always ask, not how much better off a people might be, but how much worse. Of all theological systems, the most convincing is Manicheism, which, of course, under another name, was held by the Puritans themselves. What we call Restoration morality—the morality, that is to say, of a king and court—might well have become that of the nation at large under a Stuart dynasty safe from religious revolution.

The political services of Puritanism were inestimable; they will be more feelingly remembered when England has once more to face the danger of political tyranny. I am thinking now of its effects upon social life. To it we owe the characteristic which, in some other countries, is expressed by the term English prudery, the accusation implied being part of the general charge of hypocrisy. It is said by observers among ourselves that the prudish habit of mind is dying out, and this is looked upon as a satisfactory thing, as a sign of healthy emancipation. If by prude be meant a secretly vicious person who affects an excessive decorum, by all means let the prude disappear, even at the cost of some shamelessness. If, on the other hand, a prude is one who, living a decent life, cultivates, either by bent or principle, a somewhat extreme delicacy of thought and speech with regard to elementary facts of human nature, then I say that this is most emphatically a fault in the right direction, and I have no desire to see its prevalence diminish. On the whole, it is the latter meaning which certain foreigners have in mind when they speak of English prudery—at all events, as exhibited by women; it being, not so much an imputation on chastity, as a charge of conceited foolishness. An English woman who typifies the *bégueule* may be spotless as snow; but she is presumed to have snow's other quality, and at the same time to be a thoroughly absurd and intolerable creature. Well, here is the point of difference. Fastidiousness of speech is not a direct outcome of Puritanism, as our literature sufficiently proves; it is a refinement of civilization following upon absorption into the national life of all the best things which Puritanism had to teach. We who know English women by the experience of a lifetime are well aware that their careful choice of language betokens, far more often than not, a corresponding delicacy of mind. Landor saw it as a ridiculous trait that English people were so mealy-mouthed in speaking of their bodies; De Quincey, taking him to task for this remark, declared it a proof of blunted sensibility due to long residence in Italy; and, whether the particular explanation held good or not, as regards the question at issue, De Quincey was perfectly right. It is very good to be mealy-mouthed with respect to everything that reminds us of the animal in man. Verbal delicacy in itself will not prove an advanced civilization, but civilization, as it advances, assuredly tends that way.

## XXIII.

All through the morning, the air was held in an ominous stillness. Sitting over my books, I seemed to feel the silence; when I turned my look to the window, I saw nothing but the broad, grey sky, a featureless expanse, cold, melancholy. Later, just as I was bestirring myself to go out for an afternoon walk, something white fell softly across my vision. A few minutes more, and all was hidden with a descending veil of silent snow.

It is a disappointment. Yesterday I half believed that the winter drew to its end; the breath of the hills was soft; spaces of limpid azure shone amid slow-drifting clouds, and seemed the promise of spring. Idle by the fireside, in the gathering dusk, I began to long for the days of light and warmth. My fancy wandered, leading me far and wide in a dream of summer England. . . .

This is the valley of the Blythe. The stream ripples and glances over its brown bed warmed with sunbeams; by its bank the green flags wave and rustle, and, all about, the meadows shine in pure gold of buttercups. The hawthorn hedges are a mass of gleaming blossom, which scents the breeze. There above rises the heath, yellow-mantled with gorse, and beyond, if I walk for an hour or two, I shall come out upon the sandy cliffs of Suffolk, and look over the northern sea. . . .

I am in Wensleydale, climbing from the rocky river that leaps amid broad pastures up to the rolling moor. Up and up, till my feet brush through heather, and the grouse whirrs away before me. Under a glowing sky of summer, this air of the uplands has still a life which spurs to movement, which makes the heart bound. The dale is hidden; I see only the brown and purple wilderness, cutting against the blue with great round shoulders, and, far away to the west, an horizon of sombre heights. . . .

I ramble through a village in Gloucestershire, a village which seems forsaken in this drowsy warmth of the afternoon. The houses of grey stone are old and beautiful, telling of a time when Englishmen knew how to build whether for rich or poor; the gardens glow with flowers, and the air is delicately sweet. At the village end, I come into a lane, which winds upwards between grassy slopes, to turf and bracken and woods of noble beech. Here I am upon a spur of the Cotswolds, and before me spreads the wide vale of Evesham, with its ripening crops, its fruiting orchards, watered by sacred Avon. Beyond, softly blue, the hills of Malvern. On the branch hard by warbles a little bird, glad in his leafy solitude. A rabbit jumps through the fern. There sounds the laugh of a woodpecker from the copse in yonder hollow. . . .

In the falling of a summer night, I walk by Ullswater. The sky is still warm with the afterglow of sunset, a dusky crimson smouldering above the dark mountain line. Below me spreads a long reach of the lake, steel-grey between its dim colourless shores. In the profound stillness, the trotting of a horse beyond the water sounds strangely near; it serves only to make more sensible the repose of Nature in this her sanctuary. I feel a solitude unutterable, yet nothing akin to desolation; the heart of the land I love seems to beat in the silent night gathering around me; amid things eternal, I touch the familiar and the kindly earth. Moving, I step softly, as though my footfall were an irreverence. A turn in the road, and there is wafted to me a faint perfume, that of meadow-sweet. Then I see a light glimmering in the farmhouse window—a little ray against the blackness of the great hillside, below which the water sleeps. . . .

A pathway leads me by the winding of the river Ouse. Far on every side stretches a homely landscape, tilth and pasture, hedgerow and clustered trees, to where the sky rests upon the gentle hills. Slow, silent, the river lapses between its daisied banks, its grey-green osier beds. Yonder is the little town of St. Neots. In all England no simpler bit of rural scenery; in all the world nothing of its kind more beautiful. Cattle are lowing amid the rich meadows. Here one may loiter and dream in utter restfulness, whilst the great white clouds mirror themselves in the water as they pass above. . .
.

I am walking upon the South Downs. In the valleys, the sun lies hot, but here sings a breeze which freshens the forehead and fills the heart with gladness. My foot upon the short, soft turf has an unwearied lightness; I feel capable of walking on and on, even to that farthest horizon where the white cloud casts its floating shadow. Below me, but far off, is the summer sea, still, silent, its ever-changing blue and green dimmed at the long limit with luminous noontide mist. Inland spreads the undulant vastness of the sheep-spotted downs, beyond them the tillage and the woods of Sussex weald, coloured like to the pure sky above them, but in deeper tint. Near by, all but hidden among trees in yon lovely hollow, lies an old, old hamlet, its brown roofs decked with golden lichen; I see the low church-tower, and the little graveyard about it. Meanwhile, high in the heaven, a lark is singing. It descends; it drops to its nest, and I could dream that half the happiness of its exultant song was love of England. . . .

It is all but dark. For a quarter of an hour I must have been writing by a glow of firelight reflected on to my desk; it seemed to me the sun of summer. Snow is still falling. I see its ghostly glimmer against the vanishing sky. To-morrow it will be thick upon my garden, and perchance for several days. But when it melts, when it melts, it will leave the snowdrop. The crocus, too, is waiting, down there under the white mantle which warms the earth.

## XXIV.

Time is money—says the vulgarest saw known to any age or people. Turn it round about, and you get a precious truth—money is time. I think of it on these dark, mist-blinded mornings, as I come down to find a glorious fire crackling and leaping in my study. Suppose I were so poor that I could not afford that heartsome blaze, how different the whole day would be! Have I not lost many and many a day of my life for lack of the material comfort which was necessary to put my mind in tune? Money is time. With money I buy for cheerful use the hours which otherwise would not in any sense be mine; nay, which would make me their miserable bondsman. Money is time, and, heaven be thanked, there needs so little of it for this sort of purchase. He who has overmuch is wont to be as badly off in regard to the true use of money, as he who has not enough. What are we doing all our lives but purchasing, or trying to purchase, time? And most of us, having grasped it with one hand, throw it away with the other.

## XXV.

The dark days are drawing to an end. Soon it will be spring once more; I shall go out into the fields, and shake away these thoughts of discouragement and fear which have lately too much haunted my fireside. For me, it is a virtue to be self-centred; I am much better employed, from every point of view, when I live solely for my own satisfaction, than when I begin to worry about the world. The world frightens me, and a frightened man is no good for anything. I know only one way in which I could have played a meritorious part as an active citizen—by becoming a schoolmaster in some little country town, and teaching half a dozen teachable boys to love study for its own sake. That I could have done, I daresay. Yet, no; for I must have had as a young man the same mind that I have in age, devoid of idle ambitions, undisturbed by unattainable ideals. Living as I do now, I deserve better of my country than at any time in my working life; better, I suspect, than most of those who are praised for busy patriotism.

Not that I regard my life as an example for any one else; all I say is, that it is good for me, and in so far an advantage to the world. To live in quiet content is surely a piece of good citizenship. If you can do more, do it, and God-speed! I know myself for an exception. And I ever find it a good antidote to gloomy thoughts to bring before my imagination the lives of men, utterly unlike me in their minds and circumstances, who give themselves with glad and hopeful energy to the plain duties that lie before them. However one's heart may fail in thinking of the folly and baseness which make so great a part of to-day's world, remember how many bright souls are living courageously, seeing the good wherever it may be discovered, undismayed by portents, doing what they have to do with all their strength. In every land there are such, no few of them, a great brotherhood, without distinction of race or faith; for they, indeed, constitute the race of man, rightly designated, and their faith is one, the cult of reason and of justice. Whether the future is to them or to the talking anthropoid, no one can say. But they live and labour, guarding the fire of sacred hope.

In my own country, dare I think that they are fewer than of old? Some I have known; they give me assurance of the many, near and far. Hearts of noble strain, intrepid, generous; the clear head, the keen eye; a spirit equal alike to good fortune and to ill. I see the true-born son of England, his vigour and his virtues yet unimpaired. In his blood is the instinct of honour, the scorn of meanness; he cannot suffer his word to be doubted, and his hand will give away all he has rather than profit by a plebeian parsimony. He is frugal only of needless speech. A friend staunch to the death; tender with a grave sweetness to those who claim his love; passionate, beneath stoic seeming, for the causes he holds sacred. A hater of confusion and of idle noise, his place is not where the mob presses; he makes no vaunt of what he has done, no boastful promise of what he will do; when the insensate cry is loud, the counsel of wisdom overborne, he will hold apart, content with plain work that lies nearest to his hand, building, strengthening, whilst others riot in destruction. He was ever hopeful, and deems it a crime to despair of his country. "Non, si male nunc, et olim sic erit." Fallen on whatever evil days and evil tongues, he remembers that Englishman of old, who, under every menace, bore right onwards; and like him, if so it must be, can make it his duty and his service to stand and wait.

## XXVI.

Impatient for the light of spring, I have slept lately with my blind drawn up, so that at waking, I have the sky in view. This morning, I awoke just before sunrise. The air was still; a faint flush of rose to westward told me that the east made fair promise. I could see no cloud, and there before me, dropping to the horizon, glistened the horned moon.

The promise held good. After breakfast, I could not sit down by the fireside; indeed, a fire was scarce necessary; the sun drew me forth, and I walked all the morning about the moist lanes, delighting myself with the scent of earth.

On my way home, I saw the first celandine.

So, once more, the year has come full circle. And how quickly; alas, how quickly! Can it be a whole twelvemonth since the last spring? Because I am so content with life, must life slip away, as though it grudged me my happiness? Time was when a year drew its slow length of toil and anxiety and ever frustrate waiting. Further away, the year of childhood seemed endless. It is familiarity with life that makes time speed quickly. When every day is a step in the unknown, as for children, the days are long with gathering of experience; the week gone by is already far in retrospect of things learnt, and that to come, especially if it foretell some joy, lingers in remoteness. Past mid-life, one learns little and expects little. To-day is like unto yesterday, and to that which shall be the morrow. Only torment of mind or body serves to delay the indistinguishable hours. Enjoy the day, and, behold, it shrinks to a moment.

I could wish for many another year; yet, if I knew that not one more awaited me, I should not grumble. When I was ill at ease in the world, it would have been hard to die; I had lived to no purpose, that I could discover; the end would have seemed abrupt and meaningless. Now, my life is rounded; it began with the natural irreflective happiness of childhood, it will close in the reasoned tranquillity of the mature mind. How many a time, after long labour on some piece of writing, brought at length to its conclusion, have I laid down the pen with a sigh of thankfulness; the work was full of faults, but I had wrought sincerely, had done what time and circumstance and my own nature permitted. Even so may it be with me in my last hour. May I look back on life as a long task duly completed—a piece of biography; faulty enough, but good as I could make it—and, with no thought but one of contentment, welcome the repose to follow when I have breathed the word "Finis."

Milton Keynes UK
Ingram Content Group UK Ltd.
UKHW030625061024
449204UK00004B/310

9 789362 511492